TAPATI BHARADWAJ

Rammohun Roy (1772-1833): a public intellectual and the arrival of native printed texts in India.
Mastering imperial print: acts of resistance and collaboration.

TAPATI BHARADWAJ

TAPATI BHARADWAJ

Copyright © 2014 Tapati Bharadwaj

All rights reserved.

ISBN: 8192875245
ISBN-13: 978-8192875248

TAPATI BHARADWAJ

DEDICATION
...

TAPATI BHARADWAJ

CONTENTS

	Acknowledgments	i
1	INTRODUCTION	1
2	NATIVES AND PRINT. RAMMOHUN'S USE OF THE EARLY REALM OF PRINT IN THE 1800S.	3
3	RAMMOHUN'S LOCAL AND GLOBAL REAERSHIP WITHIN THE EMERGING SOCIAL REALM OF PRINT.	21
4	CONCLUSION.	46
	APPENDICES.	53

TAPATI BHARADWAJ

TAPATI BHARADWAJ

ACKNOWLEDGMENTS

Years ago, getting to my undergraduate college on College Street, Calcutta, was an exciting experience; I have to confess that the canteen with the endless cups of tea and *adda* lured me more than the classrooms. I am grateful to the city of Calcutta that has provided me with inspiration.

TAPATI BHARADWAJ

1 INTRODUCTION.

Introduction

In the newly established realm of print culture set up by the Britishers in the last two decades of the eighteenth century, it did not take long for the natives to pick up the new technology, and the English language. This process of exchange and learning was made possible through close interaction. In fact, within a few decades, native writers in English saw their works being printed in England and reaching out both to a readership in England and India. In 1832, the London publishing house, Smith Elder and Co. published Rammohun Roy's[1] *Exposition of the Practical Operation of the Judicial and Revenue Systems of India and of the General Character and condition of its Native Inhabitants, As submitted in Evidence to the authorities in England.*[2] This work was, in part, a response to certain questions that had been raised in the English Parliament regarding the habits and conditions of India.

What is remarkable in the *Exposition* is Rammohun's thorough understanding of the European systems of political and social thought. Rammohun was largely educated within pre-colonial educational systems, which were uninfluenced by European knowledge. It was only when he started working for different officials of the East India Company from 1805 that he learned about Western systems of thinking. About his education on Western civilization he wrote in the *Exposition*:

---

[1] Throughout this chapter, I will refer to Rammohun Roy as Rammohun. For his works, I have referred to: *The English Works of Raja Rammohun Roy. Parts I - V.* ed. Dr. Kalidas Nag and Debajyoti Burman (Calcutta: Sadharon Brahmo Samaj, 1948).

[2] Rammohun Roy. *Exposition of the Practical Operation of the Judicial and Revenue Systems of India and of the General Character and condition of its Native Inhabitants, As submitted in Evidence to the authorities in England* (London: Smith Elder, 1832). This was a report that Rammohun Roy submitted to the House of Commons in England in 1831.

> From occasionally directing my studies to the subjects and events peculiarly connected with Europe, and from an attentive though partial, practical observation in regard to some of them, I felt impressed with the idea, that in Europe literature was zealously encouraged and knowledge widely diffused; that mechanics were almost in a state of perfection, and politics in daily progress; …
>
> I arrived in England on the 8th of April following. The particulars of my voyage and travels will be found in a Journal which I intend to publish.[3]

Here, Rammohun reveals his admiration for all aspects of modern Western civilization; he also reveals an awareness of himself as a public intellectual, operating in a realm of print that traveled within India and the Western worlds. Why was he was so keen to write a travelogue of his voyage to England?—Rammohun was fond of print to the point where whatever he thought about and wanted to do found its way into print. Even his theological and social disputes were worked out in print. He reveled in print, dashing off pamphlets to the printers.[4] He enjoyed the publicity that his printed works gave him, by reaching a local and a global readership. In this book, I argue that the realm of English native print in Calcutta in the early nineteenth century was dominated by the writings of Rammohun Roy. I look at how it was possible for Rammohun to operate within the newly formed communications circuit that specifically targeted the native readers. How did printing take place in Calcutta, and who were involved? How did native entrepreneurs to pick up the new technology? This book is an attempt to recuperate some sort of history of the communications circuit that was established for and by the natives in the early nineteenth century.

---

[3] Ibid., p.8.

[4] Most moderately wealthy people in Britain made use of print for semi permanent documents and official correspondence, legal notices, circulars, etc. Some still used scribes. Rammohun's use of print in this manner is clearly a Western habit, which he must have picked up as a result of his interaction with the officials of the Company for whom he worked.

RAMMOHUN ROY: A PUBLIC INTELLECTUAL.

2 NATIVES AND PRINT. RAMMOHUN'S USE OF THE EARLY REALM OF PRINT IN THE 1800S.

In the last two decades of the eighteenth century, all the printing presses were owned and operated by Europeans who hired natives as compositors and printers. Local craftsmen, carpenters and blacksmiths were needed for maintenance and repair work. These presses became teaching grounds, which made it possible for Indians to learn. 1800 marks a shift in the very system of print culture in India as printed texts began to be published for the natives. The year also saw the establishment of two institutions involved in publishing, the Srirampur Mission Press, and the College of Fort William—institutions where books were published in order to be consumed by the natives. What was the nature of the indigenous readership? New educational policies and missionary zeal were the reasons why books were printed. In the process, it became possible for new systems of knowledge to be disseminated. But was it easy for this new print technology to be accepted and mastered by the natives within Calcutta? I argue that pre-colonial Indian society had always been hybrid and pluralistic, with its Hindu and Islamic past, and this characteristic made it more amenable to accepting new ideas. An element of cosmopolitanism is evident in the lives of Rammohun and his forefathers, in a time when even high-caste Hindus would have worked with and for the Muslim rulers. Subsequently, social interaction between certain classes and communities of Indians and the Europeans became acceptable, making it possible for European knowledge to be learnt willingly by the natives.

Life of Rammohun Roy

We do not have records or personal anecdotes of what it meant for a Brahmin in the eighteenth century to work and interact, socially or professionally, with the Britishers. Was this interaction fraught with a sense of racial otherness? It would be rather reductive to write off any relationship between the natives and the Englishmen as one that was between the white ruler and the ruled. In the pre-colonial past, many Brahmins had worked for the Muslim rulers without losing their caste; in fact, they had learnt Persian, which was the language of the court, and acquired Persianised social habits that were in conformity with the ruling class. In a similar vein, working for the British would not really have been socially difficult. The life of Rammohun and his forefathers who worked for the Muslim rulers explains how so many Hindus were able to interact with the British with relative ease. Social interaction of this kind made it possible for the easy transmission of European culture and knowledge into India.

Rammohun was born in 1772 (many regard his date of birth as 1774), in Radhanagar, near Krishnanagar, in a devout Hindu family and inherited the religiosity that marked his forefathers.[5] Krishnanagar was known to be steeped in Hindu culture. His forefathers settled in Murshidabad and were in the service of the Muslim rulers. He wrote in a letter, "My ancestors were Brahmins of a high order, and from time immemorial, were devoted to the religious duties of their race, down to my fifth progenitor who about one hundred and forty years ago gave up spiritual exercises for worldly pursuits and aggrandizement."[6] His forefathers would have known Persian and Urdu. Rammohun's great grandfather, Krishnachandra Banerji, moved his family to the village of Radhanagar, opposite Krishnanagar, and worked for the Nawab of Bengal and earned the title of "Roy". This took place in the reign of Aurangzeb (1619-1707). His youngest son, Brajabinode, was placed in a high position in the court of Siraj-ud-daulah. Eventually, he left the service of the Nawab and retired. His fifth son, Ramkanta, was Rammohun's father. Ramkanta, despite being a Vaishnava, was married to a Sakta. Rammohun's maternal family belonged to the "sacerdotal order by profession as well as by birth ...[and] adhered to a life of religious observances and devotion."[7] His family was equally conversant with the ostentation of the Muslim court and the religiosity of the Hindu temple.

As a young man, Rammohun was educated in Bengali, and later Persian as the latter was the official language. We can speculate that his

---

[5] For the life of Rammohun Roy, see Sophia Dobson Collet, *The Life and Letters of Raja Rammohun Roy*, ed. Dilip Kumar Biswas and Prabhat Chandra Ganguli (Calcutta: Sadharon Brahmo Samaj, 1900). Reprint 1988.

[6] "Letter by Rammohun Roy" published by Mr. Sandford Arnot in the *Athenaeum* in London, Oct. 5, 1833, pp. 666-668; quoted in Collet, *Raja Rammohun Roy*, p. 461.

[7] Ibid., p. 461.

education would have been a model of how many young men would have been educated. He was sent to Patna to learn Arabic, where he was taught from Arabic translations of Euclid and Aristotle, the Koran, and the writings of the Sufis. Subsequently, he studied Sanskrit at Benares. About this period he wrote:

> In conformity with the usage of my paternal race, and the wish of my father, I studied the Persian and Arabic languages, these being indispensable to those who attached themselves to the courts of the Mohamaden princes, and agreeably to the usage of my maternal relations, I devoted myself to the study of the Sanskrit and the theological works written in it, which contain the body of Hindoo literature, law and religion.[8]

He studied in five different languages, namely, Sanskrit, Arabic, Persian, Urdu and Bengali. The Sanskrit and the Arabic systems of education were very different from each other, but each is seen as indispensable to the other. Rammohun reveals remarkable ease in how he was able to master these two varied systems of knowledge. If he was able to comprehend, simultaneously, two different epistemic systems, it is not surprising that subsequently he grasped the revolutionary characteristics of European, modern knowledge. Brajendranath Seal[9] and Sushobhan Sarkar[10] agree that Rammohun's greatness lies in the fact that he was able to synthesize Hindu, Islamic and Western cultures. Reverend William Yates, who was attached to the Baptist missionary wrote a letter in 1816, describing Rammohun:

> I was introduced to him about a year ago; before this, he was not acquainted with anyone who cared for his soul. ... When I first knew him he would talk only on metaphysical subjects such as the eternity of matter ... but he has lately become much more humble and disposed to converse about the Gospel. ... He visited Eustace lately and stayed to family prayer, with which he was quite delighted.[11]

---

[8] Ibid., p. 461.

[9] Brajendranath Seal, *Rammohun the Universal Man* (Calcutta: Sadharon Brahmo Samaj, 1933), pp.2-3.

[10] Susobhan Chandra Sarkar, *Notes on the Bengal Renaissance* (Bombay: Peoples Publishing House, 1946).

[11] Collet, *Raja Rammohun Roy*, p. 123.

Within a short period of time, as a result of his intimacy with the reverend Rammohun was able to learn about Christianity as it was practised. Rammohun's life allows us to understand how English thought processes were able to impress Indians, as the social and intellectual life of certain sections of India was always receptive to new ideas.

The Koran and the tenets of monotheism made an impact on Rammohun. By the age of fifteen he was critical of idolatory and left home, traveling to Tibet in order to learn about Buddhism. On his return home after a few years, around 1791-92, he was unable to reconcile himself to the beliefs of his family, and had theological disagreements with them. About this period he wrote:

> I proceeded on my travels, and passed through different countries, chiefly within, but some beyond, the bounds of Hindoostan, with a feeling of great aversion to the establishment of the British power in India. When I had reached the age of twenty, my father recalled me, and restored me to his favor; after which I first saw and began to associate with Europeans, and soon after made myself tolerably acquainted with their laws and forms of Government. Finding them generally more intelligent, more steady and moderate in their conduct, I gave up my prejudice against them and became inclined in their favor.[12]

Within his lifetime, we see the disappearance of one system of life and the emergence of the new. In the early years of his life, the British were still to establish themselves as the rulers of India; more importantly, Rammohun was yet to fully understand the nature of European knowledge. It was only when he started associating with different officials of the East India Company that he realized the modern-ness of Western civilization. By 1796 he had separated from his family, and stayed for a while in Calcutta. He also purchased property in Hooghly, which gave him a steady income. As a result of his moneylending practice he interacted with many officials of the East India Company. He left Calcutta in 1799 and traveled in north India, spending some time in Benares. He studied Sanskrit, and earned a living by copying manuscripts. His father died in 1803 and by 1805, he had started working for the East India Company as a *munshi* in Rangpur; his employer was John Digby. It was here that he started to have socio-religious discussions with his native friends. By 1814, when he moved to Calcutta, he

---

[12] "Letter," quoted in Collet, *Raja Rammohun Roy*, p. 462.

had amassed enough money to become a zamindar that allowed him an annual income of ten thousand rupees.[13] His wealth and his moneylending made him superficially indistinguishable from many of the *zamindars* who lived in Calcutta.

Rammohun, though, was different from his contemporaries. By the time he was twenty, he had broken away from the religious tradition of his father, and was thoroughly familiar with Hindu, Islamic and Buddhist systems of thought. He had started life with the intention of working for the Muslim rulers in Murshidabad, but realized that the Islamic phase of Indian history was on the wane. Rammohun himself had been deeply rooted in the cosmopolitan upper class Persian culture of the eighteenth century[14] but with the consolidation of British power in India, Rammohun and many of his generation of the early nineteenth century alienated themselves from their Islamic heritage. Moreover, English education "placed an impenetrable barrier between the nineteenth century and the immediate pre-British past, which perhaps had contained certain healthy non-conformist elements along with much that was undoubtedly ossified."[15] The absence of pre British Islamic scholarship was a result of the rapid disappearance of the knowledge of Persian, and the emergence of English historiography.[16] The Indian intelligentsia became dependent on these narratives of history, as did Rammohun. This particular mind frame which we see in Rammohun, of rejecting many aspects of the Islamic past and accepting many characteristics of Western-ness, is representative of his age. It also explains why many aspects of Western civilization, print culture in particular, were able to thrive. Printing was easily mastered by the natives as they saw the usefulness of the technology to themselves even as it was used by the rulers.

The social reasons behind the success of print

Print aided in bringing about epistemic changes within Indian society. The dissemination of English systems of education and the use of printed books was one way through which new, Western knowledge systems were introduced. The pluralism within Indian society made it possible for the

---

[13] For details on his life, see Collet, *Raja Rammohun Roy*, pp. 1-27.

[14] Sarkar, *Bengal Renaissance*, p. 19.

[15] Ibid., p. 18.

[16] Ibid., p. 20.

new, British educational policies to be successful. Printed books found an Indian readership quite easily, and the technology of print found native entrepreneurs who quickly learned the trade. Not surprisingly, Rammohun was able to learn about European systems of knowledge through his intimate relationship with some of the officials of the EIC for whom he worked.

It is easy to argue that Rammohun was unusual for his time period in the early nineteenth century; he was like, and unlike, many of his social contemporaries. Rammohun Roy was forty one years old when he settled in Calcutta, becoming a member of the nouveau riche. The milieu of rich families in Calcutta, which emerged in the early years of the East India Company, represents not merely the economic growth of a particular group of people, but also has to be seen as a new socio-cultural phenomenon. According to Chitra Deb, the wealth of the "great houses" was not based on hereditary occupations or feudal landed wealth; their roots could be traced to the city of Calcutta, in the years after 1742, during the decline of the Mughals, when Calcutta grew to become a trading center.[17] Many of the "great houses" came from the lower castes, and took up posts as intermediaries between the Indians and the British—in conducting trade, collecting debts and looking after the accounts of the EIC. Most of them won enormous wealth through private trade and usury. Rammohun had also made his wealth through usury, but he distinguished himself from this social group as he was more of a *pandit* than a *babu*.

Rammohun was well versed in Sanskrit, a scholar in his own right, and a polyglot. His personal habits were like the *bhadrolok* and yet he hankered for recognition as a shastric scholar. He was "ridiculed by the pandit establishment for imitating the outward appearance of the *ashraf* (Mughal aristocrat) which was fashionable among the *bhadrolok*; he sought scholarly recognition."[18] The *bhadroloks* were Hindus, but they were influenced by the Persianized *nawabi* culture.[19] Though Rammohun would attire himself in a

---

[17] Chitra Deb, "The Great Houses of Calcutta" *Calcutta: The Living City. Volume I: The Past*, ed. Sukanta Chaudhuri (Calcutta: Oxford University Press, 1990), pp. 56-63.

[18] Bruce Carlisle Robertson, *Raja Rammohun Roy. The Father of Modern India*. (Delhi: Oxford University Press, 1999), p. 24.

[19] Till the early nineteenth century, Hindus and Muslims participated in a common elite culture, but differed in how they reacted to British presence. Muslim response was largely negative as they were losing the positions of privilege which they had enjoyed for centuries.

nawabi manner, he was quite anglicized in his European habits, and could speak fluent English. He was described by the missionaries in the following manner:

> Rama-Mohana-Raya, a very rich Rarhee[sic] Brahmun of Calcutta, is a respectable Sanskrit scholar, and so well versed in Persian, that he is called Moulvee-Rama-Mohana-Raya: he also writes English with correctness and reads with ease—English, Mathematical and metaphysical works. He has published, in Bengalee, one or two philosophical works from the Sanskrit which he hopes may be useful in leading his countrymen to renounce idolatory. Europeans breakfast at his house, at a separate table in the English fashion; he has paid us a visit at Serampore.[20]

Rammohun was a Sanskrit scholar, who was addressed as a *maulvi*, and also conformed to the prevalent notions of caste. He had to face criticism from many regarding this contradiction between theory and practice, as evident in *Chari Prasna* (1822), printed in the *Samachar Darpan* (published by the Baptist Missionaries) to which he replied in *Chari Prasner Uttar*. He was conversant with different cultural traditions, and like his forefathers, had been given an appropriate education that would allow him to work under the Muslim rulers in Murshidabad. Eventually, with the rise of British power in India, Rammohun worked for them, and grasped the full extent of what they represented.

It was relatively easy for Rammohun to navigate between different cultural and epistemic terrains. Those living in pre-colonial, British India were participants of both Islamic and Hindu cultures. Often, this fact was elided in criticisms that were targeted at Rammohun by the self-professed upholders of Hinduism of that time. Rammohun would reply that the forefathers of the true practitioners of Hinduism had interacted intimately with the Muslims; they had served "men of an alien [Muslim] race, had used Mahomodan tooth-powder and perfume, had studied Mahomedan lore with Mahomedans, had instructed men of an alien faith" in the religious texts.[21] It was, in other words, impossible for anyone to have been unaffected by the different aspects of Islamic culture. Rammohun was aware that he belonged to such a multi-cultural tradition. He consciously chose to learn about the Britishers and interact with them, becoming

---

[20] Collet, *Raja Rammohun Roy*, p. 72.

[21] Ibid., p. 150.

proficient in the English language, and also about all the aspects of European civilization. There were few in early nineteenth century Calcutta who were so well versed in Hindu, Islamic and British cultures. When he settled in Calcutta, he was thorough in understanding what the colonizers represented, and their points of view. In an English translation, he voiced what he considered was the European point of view; he wrote: "Some Europeans endued with high principles of liberality, but unacquainted with the ritual part of Hindu idolatory are disposed to palliate it by an interpretation, which, though plausible, is by no means well founded."[22] His capacity to gauge both the native's and the non-native's points of view reveals a sensibility that distinguishes him from his contemporaries.

We tend to perceive this phenomenon of being able to move from one cultural terrain to another as modern, and a characteristic of cosmopolitanism. Rammohun was equally comfortable in different cultural contexts, and often sought out new epistemic situations. His compulsive choice to be positioned within different socio-cultural spaces was a non-violent psychical process. Even if he participated in the culture of the colonized, viewing himself through the eyes of the colonizer was not a traumatic experience. In a way, this is akin to the notion of "double consciousness," a term coined by William du Bois in describing the alienated condition of the African American living in a white dominated American society, towards the end of the nineteenth century.[23] Viewing himself from the perspective of white society made du Bois fathom his estranged condition. In *The Souls of Black Folks*, he describes how the fractured psyche of the African American came into being. Drawing upon his own experiences as a black child in a white society that did not want him, he writes that his estrangement was symptomatic of the condition of the freed slaves in antebellum United States. In his childhood, his gestures of friendship were brusquely refused "peremptorily, with a glance" and the black child was made to realize his racial difference.[24] According to Du Bois, this was the condition of the African-American, always positioned between two cultures. He described this psychical condition as also descriptive of other colonized people:

---

[22] Ibid., p. 73.

[23] William DuBois, *The Souls of Black Folks* (New York and London: Norton, 1999).

[24] Ibid., p. 10.

> After the Egyptian and Indian, the Greek and Roman, the Teuton and Mongolian, the Negro is a sort of seventh son, born with a veil, and gifted with second-sight in this American world, a world which yields him no true self-consciousness, but only lets him see himself through the revelation of the other world. It is a peculiar sensation, this double consciousness, this sense of always looking at one's self through the eyes of others, of measuring one's soul by the tape of a world that looks on in amused contempt and pity. One ever feels his twoness, an American, a Negro; two souls, two thoughts, two unreconciled strivings; two warring ideals in one dark body, whose dogged strength alone keeps it from being torn asunder.[25]

This notion of "double consciousness" is a model which explains the processes involved when one crosses over into another cultural and social system. Rammohun crossed over the cultural and epistemic borders of the Indian self and desired to transform certain aspects of Indian society by looking at it from the perspective of the English. As pre-colonial Indian society was never really homogeneous, it easily accepted the new-ness of Western civilization.

Print in Calcutta before Rammohun Roy's arrival

The stories regarding Rammohun and his intimate relation with print are not really documented, and we can only add up some of what we know to make a hypothetical whole. As a person who had spent the first twenty years of his life far away from the center of British power in Calcutta, what prompted Rammohun to move to the city at the age of forty one? It is a matter of speculation how far Rammohun would have been involved with the realm of print that existed in the early decades of the nineteenth century in Calcutta. The "communications circuit" was in its formative stages and involved both Europeans and natives. We know that when Rammohun Roy moved to Calcutta in 1814, he arrived at a city that had sprung up out of three small villages, and within a few decades had grown to become a Westernised, multi-lingual urban space. The British had utilised many aspects of Western civilization in making the city. Print technology, still in its nascent stages, had spawned a small thriving industry and till 1800, catered solely to the economic, social and cultural needs of the European community.

---

[25] Ibid. pp. 10-11.

The early years of the nineteenth century saw the emergence of numerous native-owned publishing ventures.[26] Gangakishore Bhattacharya's Bangal Gajeti Press, which was the first Bengali press owned by natives, was formed around 1818. He also started a Bengali weekly, called the *Bangal Gajeti*. He was both the printer and the publisher. But the inevitable question is: how did he learn about the technology of print? Bhattacharya had been an employee of the Srirampur Mission Press, working as a compositor.[27] He left the press and published some works at Ferris and Company in Calcutta, the most notable text being the 18th century poet, Bharatchandra's *Annadamangal Kabya* in 1816. The success of these printed works made him open an office and a bookshop; eventually he started the Bangal Gajeti Press. One of the co-owners of this press was Harachandra Roy, who was also a member of Rammohun Roy's Atmiya Sabha. Rammohun would have known Harachandra Roy, which explains how he was well informed about the activities of the printing community in Calcutta; it also explains why Rammohun was able to quickly have his treatises and polemical tracts printed. One can imagine Rammohun talking about his works to Harachandra Roy, after one of the prayer meetings at the Atmiya Sabha, and subsequently, visiting the Bangal Gajeti Press in order to oversee the printing of his works. It is no surprise that the *Bangal Gajeti* also reprinted Rammohun Roy's treatises on *sati*. The realm of print in Calcutta in the first few years of the nineteenth century—of writers, printers and publishers, sometimes in the same person—involved such a small group of people, that despite the fact that Rammohun was a new resident of the city, he came to know all the key figures, native and British, who were involved. It was only by doing so that he could engage in writing and printing his works at this early stage of print culture.

Even before settling in Calcutta in 1814, Rammohun was not innocent of the nature of printed texts. It is safe to assume that even though his education in his early years would have primarily made use of manuscripts, by the time he was working in 1805 for different officials of the East India Company, he would have also become familiar with printed books and journals, particularly as, in these days before typewriting, most Government circulars and notices were printed. Nonetheless, it was only after he moved

---

[26] See Abu Henā Mostaphā Kāmāla, *The Bengali Press and Literary Writing, 1818-31*, 1st edition. (Dacca: University Press, 1977).

[27] The Mission Press was one of the well known printing houses that printed a large number of texts in many languages and I have discussed more about it in the subsequent sections.

to Calcutta in 1814 that he gained access to the technology of print and started publishing his works; *Vedanta Grantha* (1815) and *Vedanta Sastra* (1815) were his first printed texts. These works were printed privately and were in Bengali. In many ways, what distinguishes Rammohun from his native contemporaries, who also were participating in the newly established realm of print, is his hyper-critical awareness of the characteristics of print—that mechanically reproduced printed texts could reach across to a large reading audience. While at Rangpur, in north Bengal, working for John Digby, he had familiarized himself with European political developments by reading English newspapers and journals that were subscribed to by Digby. Rammohun knew that the texts that he read would have traveled a great distance from their original place of publication in England. This fact would not have been lost on Rammohun, which made Calcutta, with its nascent print industry, an attractive city to him. He realized that he could make use of print technology to become a political and intellectual participant in the new British regime in Calcutta. Amongst the native intelligentsia of this time, Rammohun was unique as he could understand and comprehend the extent to which print worked.

Rammohun knew that the European missionaries had an advantage, namely that they understood the power of printed texts. In 1821, in *The Brahmanical Magazine or The Missionary and the Brahmun*, Rammohun described how print was used by the missionaries:

> But during the last twenty years, a body of English gentlemen, who are called missionaries, have been publicly endeavoring, in several ways to convert Hindoos and Mussalmans of this country into Christianity. The first way is that of publishing and distributing among the natives various books, large and small, reviling both religions, and abusing and ridiculing the gods and saints of the former ...[28]

According to Rammohun, these were not true missionaries, for if they had been, they would have preached in independent Muslim countries like Turkey and Persia. In Calcutta, the missionaries were part of imperialism. He drew upon the point that in Bengal, where the English were the sole rulers, "an encroachment upon the rights of her poor timid and humble

---

[28] Rammohun Roy, *The Brahmunical Magazine or The Missionary and the Brahmun. Being a Vindication of the Hindoo Religion Against the Attacks of Christian Missionaries* (Calcutta, n.p.: 1821), p. 138.

inhabitants and upon their religion could not be viewed as a justifiable act."[29] Print, through its dissemination among the native reading public, Rammohun argues, had become a means of religious persecution. The freely distributed reading material among the natives was espousing Christianity, and the natives, even if astounded by the preachings of the new religion, would have become familiar with the materiality of the printed text. Earlier, I doubt if this same group of readers would have had access to any written text. Manuscripts would have been relegated to very specific segments of the learned society, and for the most, not much used in the daily everyday lives of the common people.

By the first decade of the nineteenth century, an indigenous realm of readership had been established. Therefore, by the time Rammohun started his publications in 1815, there already existed a native community that was, to a certain degree, familiar with the materiality of the printed text. He was able to tap into all the resources of print culture that had cropped up and were available, and in the process, communicate with a large group of people. Initially, all printing presses were owned by the British and all the printing presses that operated within Calcutta were imported from England. But the technology that was behind the printing press was never limited to the British printers; in fact, it was inevitable that each printing press would become a learning school for the natives. Local craftsmen, carpenters and blacksmiths were needed for maintenance and repair work. In "The Calcutta Press," J. H. Stocqueler states that the European printers would have had Indian compositors.[30] What this implies is that the European printers unwittingly taught a new generation of indigenous printers. An instance of how letterpress technology was transferred from the English to the Indians is evident in the manner in which Bengali types were made by Charles Wilkin, an employee of the East India Company. Wilkins was assisted by a native blacksmith, Panchanan Karmakar, who excelled his master in the art. It is difficult to cut the Bengali font, when compared to the Roman font, as the Bengali script has over six hundred symbols. Improvements were made to the Bengali font, and by 1785, the Honourable Company's Press was formed, from which emerged a set of Bengali books. *Regulations for the Administration of Justice in the Courts of Dewanee Adaulut (1785), Bengal Translation of Regulations for the Administration of Justice in the*

---

[29] Ibid., p. 138.

[30] J.H. Stoqueler, "The Calcutta Press," in *Calcutta Quarterly Magazine and Review* 3(Oct. 1833): 424-425.

Fouzdarry or Criminal Courts: in Bengal, Behar, Orissa (1791) were the first books of the press.[31] It was inevitable that the realm of power would shift. The Europeans knew the art of print, and the natives learnt from them. The imperatives for starting printing presses were largely due to certain governmental educational policies and missionary zeal. Whatever the reason, it created a realm of native readership that became familiar with the materiality and conventions of print.

The Mission Press: establishing a native realm of print

By the time Rammohun settled in Calcutta in 1814, the city had seen a proliferation of printed texts in Bengali. The print industry, still functioning largely under the purview of the Britishers, had grown to address certain needs of the natives, and also involved the natives in its operations. Rammohun knew the power of the printed text, but how was he going to make use of this knowledge and also be in a position to print his own works? It was one thing to be in India and be able to read a book printed in England, fully knowing that others in England were also reading the same book, but another thing to make use of the technology of print. The presence of a flourishing Bengali print culture made it possible for Rammohun to easily make use of print technology, or for that matter, to understand the key British institutions that operated in this industry and catered to the reading needs of the natives. Rammohun was able to tap into all the resources that were present in Calcutta. Certain specific publishing institutions contributed to the growth of print in Calcutta in the first few years of the nineteenth century—the Srirampur Mission Press, the College of Fort William, and the School Book Societies. Their imperatives were not profit-motivated; in fact, printed texts for the natives were results of governmental policies or missionary zeal. This first phase of native print in Calcutta, which included journals, newspapers, pamphlets and school text books, was largely a result of educational policies.

The Srirampur Missionary Press played an important role in cultivating and establishing print for the natives. The history of the Baptist Mission and its publishing endeavor is intrinsic to any description of how print in Calcutta was democratised. This history also reveals the workings of the Company, and their deep fears. Initially, Bengali letterpress technology was mastered by Charles Wilkins who worked for the East India Company.

---

[31] One of the first books to be printed in Calcutta was Nathaniel Brassey Halhed's *Grammar of the Bengal Language* in 1778, where the author draws attention to the mechanical aspects of print technology. The book was printed in a press established by Mr. Andrews, a book seller.

Eventually, this technology was transferred to the Baptist Mission Press. Baptist missionaries had a zeal to interact with the Hindus and proselytize, permission for which was refused by the British government in order to prevent antagonism from the natives. It was, after all, only with the collaboration with the natives that the East India Company could rule in a fashion that did not lead to open rebellion. William Carey (1761-1834), a Baptist missionary, was a pioneer of sorts in his efforts to print a large number of texts in Bengali. Carey was working in Malda, in north Bengal, when he translated the Bible into Bengali. His teacher, Ramram Bose, helped him with the translations. In order to print it, Bengali fonts were needed. Reading an advertisement in the newspaper, Carey got in contact with Panchanan Karmakar, where he learnt of a foundry in Calcutta. Carey purchased a printing press for forty pounds and he set it up in Malda. His request to the London Missionary Society asking for more missionaries was granted, and he was joined by others in 1799, who urged him to reside in Srirampur, a Danish enclave and outside the East India Company's jurisdiction. Carey, along with the other missionaries, formed the Baptist Mission in 1800 and in order to make a functional printing press, was joined by Karmakar in the same year. Karmakar was assisted by another craftsman and a pupil of Charles Wilkins, Manohar. He made punches of more than twelve Indian languages, and also of Chinese. It was here that the New Testament was printed in 1801. Biblical texts were translated and printed, and tracts were disseminated among the people. They were assisted in these works by pandits.

Indian pandits attached to the Baptist Mission Press also printed books of fiction in Bengali, and can thus be described as the first writers in Bengali who had their works printed. A few decades previously, this same group of pandits would have used manuscripts, but now were turning their efforts to print technology. Rammohun Roy was familiar with this group of writers, and undoubtedly would have learned the processes that were involved in writing books for printing houses. *Pratapaditya Charita*, a biography of King Pratapaditya of Jessore, was published in July, 1801, and was written by Ramram Basu. Golaknath Sarma translated the Sanskrit *Hitopadesa* in 1802. *Batris Simhasan* was published by Mrityunjay Tarkalankar in the same year. 1802 also saw publication of Ramram Basu's *Lipimala, or the Bracelet of Writing*. In 1805, Chandicharan Munshi came out with a Bengali translation of the Persian *Tutinama*, titled *Tota Itihas*. Rajiblochan Mukhopadhyay published a biography of Raja Krishna Chandra of Nadia, *Maharaj Krshnachandra Rayasya Charitram* in the same year. The year 1808 saw Mrityunjay Vidyalankar publish two more books, namely *Rajabali*, a history of India till the British presence and a translation of the Sanskrit *Hitopadesa*. The Mission Press was, thus, also involved in printing books that were not meant for proselytisation.

School Book Society and educational policies

Even though the Missionary Press generated a large quantity of pamphlets and tracts for proselytisation, it was also involved in printing text books— readers, grammar books and dictionaries—for the College of Fort William and other educational institutions. For example, the Calcutta School Book Society had some of its texts printed from the Srirampur Mission Press. The Calcutta School Book Society was established in 1817, and the School Book Society in 1818. Their aim was to provide native children with texts in the vernacular. The object of the Society was the "preparation, publication and cheap or gratuitous supply of works useful in Schools and seminaries of Learning."[32] The antecedents of the School Book Society can be found in certain developments in England, where the first few decades of the nineteenth century formed the age of "philanthropy of education." Mass education was relegated to the responsibility of private charities. The policies and practices of the School Book Society were "tied up with the prevalent colonialist ideals."[33] The School Book Societies had the patronage of local intellectuals like Radhakanta Deb, Ramcomul Sen and Mrityunjay Tarkalankar, alongside the European officials and scholars in the College of Fort William. Between 1817 and 1821, the Srirampur Mission Press printed 47, 946 copies of twelve books in different languages for the Calcutta School Book Society.

That over a span of a mere twenty years, printed texts became widespread was a result of educational practices. Within these few years, the very nature of what comprised education changed, and it was only possible as a result of the availability of printed texts. A generation of new students was brought up within this system, reading text books and journals. The Srirampur Mission Press also brought out a Bengali periodical called *Digdarsan, The Indian Youth Magazine* from April 1818. The journal avoided controversial issues pertaining to religion or politics, and laid emphasis on various academic subjects—history, geography and commerce. For example, the first issue covered the following subjects—the discovery of America, the geographical limits of Hindustan, trade of Hindustan, Mr.

---

[32] Tithi Bhattacharya, *Powers of Print* (Calcutta: Oxford University Press, 2007).

[33] Ibid., p. 75.

Sadler's Journey in a Balloon, and Mount Vesuvius.[34] The Calcutta School Book Society subscribed to a thousand copies of each of the first three issues; the society also requested the editor of the journal to bring out both Bengali and English versions of the journal. By 1821, the Society had purchased 61, 250 copies of the *Digdarshan* in all the three editions.[35] If it were not for print, educational changes would not have taken place. By the 1820s, Bengali prose and syntax, along with an established realm of printers and booksellers had come into being mainly for the natives. What is of relevance is that Rammohun made use of this established realm of print to publish his texts.

In *Powers of Print*, Tithi Bhattacharya argues that printing was made use of by the British imperial state towards educating the natives. Imparting education to the colonies was a part of the capitalist notion of progress, and also intrinsic to the moral agenda that defined the impetus behind the civilizing mission of the colonial powers. Moreover, she argues that the needs of the imperial state were in keeping with the agenda of the missionaries, as evident in the establishment of the College of Fort William, and the Calcutta School Book Societies. But I doubt as to whether we can describe all the educational policies as colonial practices, meant to aid the British state in its civilizing agenda. Such a dichotomous relationship, of civilizing colonial power and passive natives, is not an effective description of the fact that the natives fell in love with the new European knowledge systems that were being introduced. In fact, in the initial years of rule, the British were interested in maintaining the indigenous schools.

Before Macaulay's absolute diktat in 1835, there was no clear cut principle that the British government followed in its educational policies towards the Indians. The social history of the first two decades of the nineteenth century reveals contradictory ideologies; while the British government seemed keen to perpetuate the indigenous, traditional educational systems in Bengal, there were many Indians who were quite against it, the most vociferous being Rammohun Roy. In an address in Fort William, in 1811, Lord Minto summarized his plans for setting up Sanskrit Colleges in Tirhut and Nadia.[36] As science and literature were "in a

---

[34] Abu Henā Mostapha Kāmāla, *The Bengali Press and Literary Writing, 1818-31*, 1st edition (Dacca: University Press, 1977), p. 41.

[35] Ibid., p. 24.

[36] "Appendix D. Lord Minto's Minute on Sanskrit College in Tirhut and Nuddea. Fort

progressive state of decay among the natives of India," his apprehension was that unless the "government interpose[d] with a fostering hand, the revival of letters" would "shortly become hopeless from a want of books or of persons capable of explaining them." Learning was the responsibility of the kings and in their decline, so had royal patronage towards education. Therefore, according to Lord Minto, the British government should not fail "to extend its fostering care to the literature of the Hindus and to aid in opening to the learned in Europe the repositories of that literature." Dissemination of knowledge would enable the prevention of crime. Teachers and professors would be appointed, alongside librarians. A public library would be "attached to each of the colleges ... with a small establishment of servants for the care of manuscripts"; moreover, "ready access [would] be afforded to both the teachers and the students, and likewise to strangers ... for the purpose of consulting, transcribing the books, or making extracts from them."[37] These were indeed grand plans. The emphasis was on ensuring the continuation of Indian learning.

There was an equally strong native lobby that vouched for the introduction of Western education. In a letter to Lord Amherst, in 1823, Rammohun voiced his criticism towards the government in its decisions to open a Sanskrit College.[38] In fact, he hoped that the English government would devote the money for education and towards "employing European Gentlemen of talents and education to instruct the natives of India in Mathematical, Natural Philosophy, Chemistry, Anatomy and other useful sciences, which the Nations of Europe have carried to a degree of perfection."[39] To Rammohun, there was little merit in continuing with the indigenous system of education. A large amount of time was spent in learning the Sanskrit language, and the "learning concealed in [it?] under the almost impervious veil" was "far from sufficient to reward the labour of acquiring it"; if the aim was to promote the language of Sanskrit, he argued, it could be done so by granting allowances to the teachers.[40] It was of little

---

William. 6 March, 1811." *Selections from Unpublished Records of Government for the Years 1748-1767 inclusive. Relating mainly to the Social Condition of Bengal. Vol. 1*, ed. Rev. J. Long (Calcutta: Office of the Superintendent of Government Printing, 1869).

[37] Ibid., pp. 554-560.

[38] "Letter of Rammohun Roy to Lord Amherst," *The Life and Letters of Raja Rammohun Roy*, ed. Sophia Collett.

[39] Ibid., p. 422.

[40] Ibid., p. 422.

use to encourage young men to spend the "most valuable period of their lives in acquiring the niceties of the Byakarun or Sanskrit Grammar."[41] Moreover, improvement of the mind could not take place from studying the issues of the Vedanta: "In what manner is the soul absorbed into the deity? What relation does it bear to the divine essence?"[42] Central to native education was the study of Vedantic doctrines which Rammohun summarized as:

> all visible things have no real existence; that as father, brother, etc. have no actual entity, they consequently deserve no real affection, and therefore, the sooner we escape from them and leave the world the better. Again, no essential benefit can be derived by the student of the Meemangsa from knowing what it is that makes the killer of a goat sinless by pronouncing certain passages of the Veds.
>
> Again the student of the Nyaya Shastra cannot be said to have improved his mind after he has learned it into how many ideal classes the objects in the Universe are divided, and what speculative relation the soul bears to the body, the body to the soul, the eye to the ear, etc.[43]

Sanskrit education, in other words, would keep the country in "darkness." Education of this kind was dependent on rote learning, and manuscripts were used. In order to change the very nature of such a system and the fundamental underlying principles, the establishment of schools, and the dissemination of printed textbooks were essential. Eventually, colonial educational practices were successful as print made it possible for books to be disseminated.

---

[41] Ibid., p. 423.

[42] Ibid., p. 423.

[43] Collet, *Raja Rammohun Roy*, p. 423.

TAPATI BHARADWAJ

3 RAMMOHUN'S LOCAL AND GLOBAL REAERSHIP WITHIN THE EMERGING SOCIAL REALM OF PRINT.

Introduction

Rammohun was involved in the realm of print culture in Calcutta in its incipient stage. He knew the power of the global printed text, and its capacity to travel across to unknown places and people. Even if we do not consider his Bengali writings, his English writings reveal an amazing degree of fluency with the nature of print culture. The readership of his English works was a large one, spread across different groups of people all across the English-speaking world. This characteristic of being aware of how to engage with different readers is what makes him unique. He was very conscious of his readership, and aware of what was needed from him as a native writer, writing for natives and for Europeans. For example, *The Precepts of Jesus, the Guide to Peace and Happiness; extracted from the Books of the New Testament ascribed to the four Evangelists. With translations into Sanskrit and Bengali*[44] was published in Calcutta in 1820. The irony was and is not lost. Here was a Hindu native, writing exegetical commentaries on the Bible. The readership would have undoubtedly been the European missionaries residing in and around Calcutta. In 1821, it was reprinted in America. Many of Rammohun's works that were published from Calcutta were reprinted in England and in America. In a letter that he wrote to a gentleman in Baltimore from Calcutta, in 1822, the note of sarcasm is obvious as he describes himself as a defender of Christianity, and the missionaries as practicing heathen doctrines:

---

[44] Raja Rammohun Roy. *The Precepts of Jesus, the Guide to Peace and Happiness; extracted from the Books of the New Testament ascribed to the four Evangelists. With translations into Sanskrit and Bengali.* (Calcutta, 1820). Reprinted in *The English Works of Raja Rammohun Roy. Part V*, pp. 3-54.

> I have now every reason to hope that the truths of Christianity will not be much longer kept hidden under the veil of heathen doctrines and practices, gradually introduced among the followers of Christ since many lovers of truth are zealously engaged in rendering the religion of Jesus clear from corruption.
>
> I admire the zeal of the Missionaries sent to this country, but disapprove of the means they have adopted. In the performance of their duty, they always begin with such obscure doctrines as are calculated to excite ridicule instead of respect, towards the religion which they wish to promulgate. The accompanying pamphlets called *The Brahmunical Magazine* and published by a Brahmun, are a proof of my assertion. The last number of this publication has remained unanswered for twelve months.[45]

Fundamental to our understanding of how English print operated in the early years of the nineteenth century is the fact that print shapes social relations. Rammohun was quite central in this process of Indians using print to engage with and against the newly established realm of the Britishers.

Social revolutions are dependent on print. The French Revolution, as Robert Darnton points out, was a result of the printing press—without the press, a group of men could "conquer the Bastille" but they could not "overthrow the Old Regime."[46] Printed texts, in the form of journals, almanacs, pamphlets, posters, pictures moulded the imagination of twenty six million French people during the Revolution. Drawing attention to the potential of the printing press, Robert Darnton wrote that the French "revolutionaries knew what they were doing when they carried printing presses in their civic processions and when they set aside one day in the revolutionary calendar for the celebration of public opinion."[47] Without print culture, runs Darnton's central argument, the French Revolution of

---

[45] "Letter," Calcutta; Oct. 27, 1822. In *The English Works of Raja Rammohun Roy. Part IV*, pp. 85-86.

[46] Robert Darton, *The Kiss of Lamourette. Reflections in Cultural History* (New York: Norton, 1990), p. xiii.

[47] Ibid., pp. xiii-xiv.

1789 would not have been possible.

Socio-political relations were redefined in the early years of the nineteenth century and print was intrinsic to these transformations. In this chapter, my specific focus is on the English writings of Rammohun, and how he used print to engage with different groups of readers. We get a glimpse of the nature of different kinds of readership. The realm of native socio-religious intellectualism in the first few years of the nineteenth century in Calcutta was going through a phase of transition. This change is made clear if we look at the life of Rammohun; in his early years, he was well versed in Persian and Islamic theology. Subsequently, with the gradual political rise of the East India Company, the politics of the dominant Islamic past changed. As Hinduism became of immense interest to the Christian missionaries and Orientalist scholars, Rammohun thought it essential to engage with Hindu theology to combat their Westernised interpretations. The native Hindu intellectual community comprised both learned pandits and *babu* scholars. There were many Sanskrit pandits at that time, more learned than Rammohun. The list of *pandits* attached to the College of Fort William (1801) reveals the names of some of the existing scholars: the chief pandit was Mrityunjay Tarkalankar, the second pandit was Ramnath Vachaspati. Mrityunjay Tarkalankar was the finest scholar of Sanskrit in Bengal. Similarly, there were many rich, educated Bengalis, like Radhakanta Deb, who were patrons of knowledge. All of them were involved in print, writing polemical tracts. Rammohun inhabited such a realm of print, which involved both natives and Europeans. The different groups of people that Rammohun was addressing can be categorised in the following manner: native intelligentsia/ pandits, rich babus, non native intelligentsia, missionaries, East India company administrators and religious ministers in England and America. Thus, by mastering the conventions of print and by learning English he was able to address the Britishers on an equal footing. In fact, his English works were meant for a non native readership, to the point where he homogenised Hinduism and defined it as it was perceived by the Britishers and the Orientalist scholars.

The *Tohfat*: Rammohun's first printed works and the realm of Persian print

Rammohun entered the realm of print culture at a time in history when there were few native editors, writers and printers involved. That he did make use of print at a time when printed texts were still new amongst the natives reveals his capacity to absorb and make use of new technologies. His first published work, *Tohfat 'l-muwahhidin*, was in Persian—as Bengali was yet to become the language of intellectual discourse—and printed in

Murshidabad around 1803, where he was working as the private munshi for Thomas Woodford.[48] Thomas Woodford was the registrar of the Appellate Court at Murshidabad at that time. It is not easy to gauge how it could have been printed in Murshidabad. We know little about his intended readership, but an examination of the text makes it evident that it would have had to be a literate one, and would have been one that was familiar with an Islamic educational system. The *Tohfat* is a theological tract on monotheism and strongly condemns idolatry. In the *Tohfat*, Rammohun states that his own religion was a mix of the different religious traditions that were prevalent in India. What becomes evident is that Rammohun's education was an Islamic one and many have commented upon his style of argumentation. According to Abid U. Ghazi:

> Roy's writing is clearly that of a Madrasa stylist, naturally fluent in the use of Arabic technical and literary vocabulary acceptable in Persian. He uses Persian couplets, Qur'anic verses, and Arabic and Persian idioms to embellish his expression. Such could be acquired over years of study, training and acquaintance with all aspects of Muslim culture. … He uses the entire armory of Islamic logic to support his ideas, which themselves are ultimately turned against the tenet of all established religions, especially Islam.[49]

His subsequent theological and socio-political writings, for which we know him, reveal little influence of his knowledge of Islamic theology. Bruce Robertson states that Rammohun did not know the Upanishads at this stage in his "intellectual development," and this work is of little importance for the study of his later religion.[50] Subsequently, Rammohun educated himself in other languages and religious traditions. What is still a matter of speculation is as to how Rammohun was able to print his works in Murshidabad. This is something we know little about. Is it possible that Rammohun sent his work to Calcutta? Did some printer carry a press to Murshidabad? Were there others involved? What was the nature of the

---

[48] For a detailed analysis, see Bruce Carlisle Robertson, *Raja Rammohun Roy, The Father of Modern India*, pp. 24-30.

[49] Abid. U. Ghazi; cited in Robertson, *Raja Rammohun Ray*, pp. 26-28.

[50] Robertson, *Raja Rammohun Roy*, pp. 25, 30.

print industry or was the text a result of a solitary printer churning out translations from Persian manuscripts? Was Rammohun able to print the *Tohfat* as a result of his intimacy with Woodford who would have known the printers in Calcutta? In fact, we know more about the realm of Persian print in Calcutta than we do about the realm of print in Murshidabad.

A parallel world of printers that catered to the needs of the Britishers existed in Calcutta; these were publishers who were printing works in Persian and other native languages, apart from also printing in English. It might be possible that Rammohun was aware of these printers through Woodford, for whom he was working in Murshidabad, but we really cannot say for sure. Only Britishers would have had access to Persian fonts and the printing presses. By the late 1780s, most printing presses would have had fonts in different languages. The most well known type foundry was established by Charles Wilkins who was attached to the Honourable Company's Press. It was in Malda, where the Company's press was initially situated, and it was here that Wilkins perfected the Persian types. There were a few other foundries that established expertise in producing Oriental fonts as these types were not easily available for import from Europe. The most successful commercial foundry that was set up was by Daniel Stuart and John Cooper who supplied to the Chronicle Press.[51] By early 1787, they had produced fonts in Bengali and Persian which were used for vernacular notices in the *Calcutta Chronicle*. The editors described their endeavors in the following manner:

> The proprietors of this Paper have been indefatigable in their endeavors to complete their assortments of types; and they have at length the satisfaction to declare, that their endeavors have proved successful even beyond their own expectations. Although they accomplished one principal object of their wishes (that of cutting and casting types of any one character or language, under their own inspection), they are enabled to print on more moderate terms than were ever accepted, or offered, in this part of the world. They entertain hopes, that the trouble they have had, in instructing the natives in the several branches of their profession, will not only be recompensed by the liberal encouragement of the public, but also become of general utility; in as much, as the circulation of works, in

---

[51] For more see Graham Shaw, *Printing in Calcutta To 1800, A Description and Checklist of Printing in Late 18th Century Calcutta* (London: The Bibliographical Society, 1981), pp. 29-38.

the Oriental languages, is now, by their endeavors, rendered more easy, from being executed at near one half of the expense heretofore attending to it.[52]

The "public" referred to was no doubt European. The easy accessibility of fonts made it possible for the circulation of works in native languages. Natives did not feature as readers of these works that were printed in "Oriental languages." The intended readership was clearly European. The printers hoped that the fonts would encourage the natives to publish. We are not sure if Rammohun would have had contact with this group of European scholars and printers at this stage of his life. The *Tohfat*, on the other hand, was meant for an exclusive native readership. This book was in keeping with other Persian writings by native scholars of this time, and most unlike the works that were printed by the Orientalist scholars.

There was a community of Britishers who, for reasons of commerce or for scholarship, was interested in bringing out printed texts in Indian languages. Francis Gladwin makes this clear in his quarterly journal, the *Asiatic Miscellany*, which he started in 1785. He wrote that the "design of the Asiatick Miscellany" would contain original works in native languages:

> Some gentlemen have promised, and others have actually supplied us with some genuine extracts from Persian authors of repute, translated with so much care, as to admit of being published with the original and translation on opposite pages. And though this part of the Work may, at first, seem particularly designed for those who study the Persian language and will undoubtedly be of singular use to them, it is yet by no means on their account alone, that the extracts appear in that form. The translations will, we trust, be always matter of curiosity and entertainment to English readers also, who in seeing them accompanied by their respective originals, will have reason to be satisfied, that what is presented to them as [a] specimen of eastern history or composition, is neither spurious nor disguised by borrowed ornament, but is genuine, pure and unadulterated.[53]

---

[52] *Calcutta Chronicle*. 26th July (1787): 1.

[53] *The Asiatik Miscellany*, cited in Thankappan Nair, *A History of the Calcutta Press* (Calcutta: Firma KLM, 1987), pp. 116-117.

Gladwin makes it clear that in his Persian writings he was targeting a readership that was specifically non native and interested in "unadulterated" native texts. His notion of the public included those who were interested in Persian, and even those Englishmen who would be "entertained" by the "genuine, pure" fonts.

Rammohun would have been well read in the works that were printed in Gladwin's journal;[54] but his readership for the *Tohfat*, on the other hand, was specifically native. One can hypothesize that his realm of readers was based in Murshidabad, and was very literate in Islamic theology. The realm of Persian readers that Gladwin was targeting was very different from the realm or readers within which Rammohun was situated. Yet, soon, the world of Rammohun would embrace the world of Gladwin and Rammohun would be targeting the same readers that Gladwin was writing for. The center of power was changing, and Rammohun was aware of this. Conforming to the dominant Islamic worldview was no longer in fashion. Rammohun turned his attention to writing in English, and soon had a readership that included officials of the East India Company, Englishmen not connected to the government, missionaries, and even readers in England and in America.

Rammohun and his English readership

In the first two decades of the nineteenth century, Rammohun worked on translating the Vedantic texts. In 1815, he translated the Vedas into Bengali; in 1816-1817, he wrote the *Abridgement of the Vedanta* in English, Bengali and Hindusthani, and translated the Upanishads into English and Bengali.[55] Rammohun was supremely aware of his readership, and churned out Bengali and English translations with great rapidity. He was able to move between different "publics". About this period of activity, he wrote:

> I have found the doctrines of Christ more conducive to moral principles, and better adapted for the use of rational beings, than any others … and have also found Hindus in general more superstitious and miserable, both in performance of their religious rites and in their domestic

---

[54] For more on the nature of works printed in the *Asiatik Miscellenary*, and the other translated Persian works, see Nair, *A History*, pp. 117-165.

[55] For more on this period of activity (1815-1820), see Sophia Dobson Collet, *The Life and Letters of Raja Rammohun Roy*, pp. 60-117.

concerns, than the rest of the known nations on the earth;
I therefore, ... translated their most revered theological
work, namely Vedant, into Bengali and Hindusthani, and
also several chapters of the Ved... I however, in the
beginnings of my pursuit, met with the greatest of
opposition from their self interested leaders, the Brahmins,
and was deserted by my nearest relations; I consequently
felt extremely melancholy; in that critical situation, the only
comfort that I had was the consoling and rational
conversation of European friends, specially those in
England and Scotland.[56]

The realm of readers for his English works comprised Europeans; no natives before him had written for such a readership, and therefore, there was no precedence as to what was expected from him as a native writer, writing in English for the Europeans. He was not hesitant in condemning the Brahmins, referring to them in the third person and in the process separating himself from the community of Hindus, and even voicing appreciation at how he had been received by the Europeans. In most ways, he was a native cultural mediator, making the east and his own culture comprehensible to the European reader.

His English works on the Vedanta are as follows: *Translation of an Abridgement of the Vedanta (1816), Translation of the Kena Upanishad (1816), Translation of the Isopanishad (1816), Translation of the Mundaka Upanishad (1819), Translation of the Katha Upanishad (1819)*. It is interesting to speculate on the need for such translations as the English-speaking world would already have been familiar with the Vedantic works of William Jones. In the preface to the *Translation of the Kuth Opunishud of the Ujoor Veda*,[57] Rammohun makes it very clear as to why he wrote these translations:

I had some time ago the satisfaction of publishing a
translation of the Katha-Upanishad of the Yajur-veda into
Bengalee; and of distributing copies of it as widely as my
circumstances would allow for the purposes of diffusing
Hindoo scriptural knowledge among the adherents of that

---

[56] "Letter to John Digby, written in 1816," Ibid., pp. 78-79.

[57] "Preface to the Translation of the Kuth-Opunishud of the Ujoor Ved," in *The English Works of Raja Rammohun Roy. Part II*, pp. 21-38.

> religion. The present publication is intended to assist the European community in forming their opinion respecting Hindoo Theology.⁵⁸

This statement is revealing, drawing attention to the nature of print in its early years, and how Rammohun made use of the power of print. William Jones and the scholars of the East India Company had worked with Hindu pandits in explaining the nature of eastern religion to the West; the Baptist missionaries had also spread their version of Hinduism by deriding it.⁵⁹ Rammohun wanted to combat these renditions of Hinduism. As we unwrap Rammohun's comment on why he had published these translations, we learn about the nature of his intended English and native readership, and the reasons why his works were important. First of all, he makes it clear that his native, Bengali-reading readers were not well versed in his version of Hinduism; therefore, he made use of a strategy that was quite expensive and he must have picked up from the missionaries—free distribution of pamphlets among the Bengali speaking Hindus so that they could improve their "scriptural knowledge". The missionaries were busy doing something similar and were also disseminating tracts in Bengali, but their focus was on ridiculing Hindu practices. The missionaries described Hinduism as originating from the devil,⁶⁰ and Rammohun, on the other hand, proclaimed that his agenda was on teaching scriptural Hinduism to the Hindus. On the other hand, the English translations were meant for the Europeans who would to some degree have been familiar with the translations of William Jones' version of Hinduism. Rammohun was a native, explaining his own religious systems to the Europeans and his credibility lay in this fact. He was almost a *pandit* who was well versed in the ways of the Europeans and made sense of the new systemic and institutional changes that were taking place.

In the English translations, Rammohun was very conscious of his readership. In an "Introduction" to one of the translations, he wrote in 1823:⁶¹

---

⁵⁸ Ibid., p. 23.

⁵⁹ For more see Collet, *Life and Letters*, p. 146.

⁶⁰ Ibid., p. 146.

⁶¹ "Translation of the Cena Upanishad, one of the chapters of the Sama Veda," in *The English Works of Raja Rammohun Roy. Part II*, pp. 13-20.

> It is with no ordinary feeling that I have already seen many respectable persons of my countrymen, to the great disappointment of their spiritual guides, rise superior to their original prejudices, and enquire into the truths of religion. As many European gentlemen, specially those who interest themselves in the improvement of their fellow-creatures, may be gratified with a view of the doctrines of the original work, it appeared to me that I might best contribute to that gratification, by translating a few chapters of the Veda into the English language, which I have accordingly done, and now submit them to their candid judgment. Such benevolent people will, perhaps, rise from a perusal of them with the conviction that in the most ancient times the inhabitants of this part of the globe ... were not unacquainted with metaphysical subjects;[62]

The European readers would understand that in ancient India, many were familiar with abstruse metaphysical theology, and that Hinduism was not only defined by ritualistic idolatory. Elsewhere, in his *Translation of the Ishopanishad*,[63] one of the chapters of the *Yajur Vedas*, he commented upon the necessity of translating such religious works into English; it was meant to educate the "Europeans, imbued with high principles of liberality, but unacquainted with the ritual part of Hindu idolatry."[64] He wrote in 1816:

> In pursuance of my vindication, I have to the best of my abilities translated this hitherto unknown work, as well an abridgement thereof, into the Hindoostanee and Bengalee languages, and distributed them, free of cost, among my own countrymen, as widely as circumstances have possibly allowed. The present is an endeavor to render an abridgement of the same into English, by which to prove to my European friends, that the superstitious practices which deform the Hindoo religion have nothing to do with

---

[62] Ibid., pp. 13-14.

[63] "Translation of the Ishopanishad, one of the Chapters of the Yajur Veda," in *The English Works of Raja Rammohun Roy. Part II*, pp. 41-55.

[64] Ibid., p.44.

the pure spirit of its dictates!⁶⁵

Rammohun took it upon himself to educate his European friends about Hinduism, using phrases and a terminology that was similar to Christianity. Hindu *pandits* had assisted the East India Company scholars in their translations, but were never accorded the same kind of relevance as were the scholars of the Company. For example, Hastings realized the need for Indian languages, and was himself well versed in Urdu and Persian. He was assisted by a group of scholarly administrators—Charles Wilkins (1750-1836), N. B. Halhed (1751-1830), J. Duncan (1756-1794) and William Jones (1746-1794). Their Orientalist knowledge greatly helped in the functioning of the administration, and also created an atmosphere for scholarship. And yet, we know little about the pandits who helped them. This lacuna was filled up by Rammohun who ensured that the works of natives were well acknowledged and publicised. In fact, he was so conscious of his English readership that he defined Hinduism as it was perceived by the Orientalist scholars. Sushoban Sarkar makes a similar case when he argues that the religion Rammohun formed, Brahmo-ism, also was largely elitist and never a popular religion as it failed to link up with the popular lower-caste monotheistic cults" that were numerous in eighteenth century Bengal, particularly in Nadia-Murshidabad.⁶⁶

Rammohun's translations: early 19th century Calcutta

Rammohun's Vedantic works can be described as the first Vedantic commentaries in a vernacular that were written for a non-Hindu, non-Sanskrit speaking readership.⁶⁷ He was aware of this as draws attention to this fact in *A Defence of Hindoo Theism*, "I must remark, however, that there is no translation of the Vedas into any of the modern languages of Hindoostan with which I am acquainted."⁶⁸ His works are exegeses on the commentaries of Shankaracharya and have a precedence in Baladeva Bidyabhusan's *Govindabhasya* and *Isabhasya*, which were the first Bengali commentaries that were written in the eighteenth century. The only

---

⁶⁵ "Translation of an Abridgement of The Vedant establishing the Unity of the Supreme Being," in *The English Works of Raja Rammohun Roy. Part II*, pp. 59-60.

⁶⁶ Susobhan Chandra Sarkar, *On the Bengal Renaissance*, p. 17.

⁶⁷ For more see Robertson, *Raja Rammohun Roy*, pp. 30-31.

⁶⁸ *A Defence of Hindoo Theism. In Reply to the Attack of an Advocate for Idolatory in Madras. 1817*. In *The English Works of Raja Rammohun Roy. Part II*, p. 85.

exception was Dara Shukoh's translations two hundred years ago around 1641. Dara Shukoh was the oldest son of Jahangir, and attracted a liberal courtly crowd of scholars, imperial officers and nobles who followed the eclectic ideology of Akbar. He was a follower of Mullah Mir (d. 1635) and Mullah Shah Badeshi (d. 1661), two important Sufi teachers. He was firmly convinced that the Upanishads preached monotheism, in a similar fashion as did Islam. With the help of Brahmin scholars whom he invited from Benares, he translated fifty two Upanishads and titled the work *Sirr-i-Akbar*. In 1671, a French traveler to India named Francis Bernier returned to France with a copy of the Persian *Upanishads*, which were translated into Latin by Duperron and titled *Oupnek'hat*. It is not clear if William Jones knew this work when he, with his group of Benares *pandits*, translated the *Isa Upanishads* in 1799. He was assisted in his works by Hindu *pandits*, but none of their names are featured in the published works. In the early years of the nineteenth century, Rammohun, as a result of his familiarity with the officials of the East India Company and the Baptist missionaries, would have known about the works of William Jones and his collaborative use of pandits.[69] The reading domain within which Rammohun worked was already inhabited by European Orientalist scholars. It is almost as if Rammohun was challenging these scholars and their lack of acknowledgement of native support. His readers were the same as those of the Orientalist scholars. Here was an instance of a *pandit* who had turned Orientalist scholar.

Rammohun had a Western readership that was denied to all natives at that time. Native pandits were not referred to by the Western world. What distinguishes Rammohun is the fact that he was also considered to be an expert on the subject of Hinduism by the Western scholars.[70] This is evident if we look at H. Wilson's lecture "Two Lectures on the Religious Practices and Opinions of the Hindus."[71] Wilson was professor of Sanksrit in Oxford and his lecture was an attempt to summarize the popular practices of the Hindus.[72] According to Wilson, it was important to know the existing philosophies and institutions of the Hindus in order to

---

[69] See Robertson's *Raja Rammohun Ray* for more on this; pp. 10-54.

[70] Ibid., pp. 55-73.

[71] H. Wilson, *Essays and Lectures on the Religions of the Hindus* (New Delhi: APS Reprint, 1976).

[72] Ibid., p.40.

comprehend them; to "overturn their errors we must know what they are."[73] Wilson cited two sources: H. T. Colebrook, who was an authority on the history of the shastras and the philosophical systems,[74] and Rammohun Roy. Rammohun was portrayed as a reformer who was changing the existing decaying systems.[75] Otherwise, Indian scholars were not recognised, and not even Mrityunjay Tarkalankar was seen as an equal by William Carey. In the *Times*, Rammohun's translations also received good reviews:

> It will be recorded as one of the remarkable incidents of the nineteenth century, that a Brahman of respectable rank and strong powers, thoroughly conversant with his own vernacular and classical literature, and almost equally familiar with the learning of the west, should have been the first to transfer into our own language ... an appreciable portion of these works."[76]

Rammohun was able to reach out to a readership that was Western as he was "equally familiar" with the West and with Islamic and Hindu scholarship. It was not hard for him to receive acclaim in the West; Wilhelm Traugott Krug, Schopenhauer and Schelling cited him. Max Mueller wrote that he was "the first who came from East to West, the first to join hands and to complete that world-wide circle through which henceforth, like an electric current, Oriental thought could run to the West and Western thought return to the East."[77] His capacity to understand the needs of his readership made it possible for him to address Western readers. He did not homogenise his readership, being fully aware that an English readership was different from a native one. The notion of the author was a new concept within India, and more so was a native writing to the English in English.

---

[73] Ibid., p. 40.

[74] H. T. Colebrooke, *Essays on the History, Literature and Religions of Ancient India* (New Delhi: Cosmo Publications, reprint 1977).

[75] Wilson also mentioned Ramacandra Vidyavagis and Prassana Kumar Thakur as examples of the new breed of Hindus; *Essays*, pp. 52-53.

[76] *The Times*. 2 October (1832), Cited in Robertson, *Raja Rammohun Roy*, p. 66.

[77] F. Max Muller, *Biographical Essays* (London: Longmans, Green, 1884), p. 13.

Theological debate in print

Rammohun's brand of Hinduism and commentaries on the Bible were unfavourably received by many, and often his critics would target him using printed tracts. Rammohun had ready answers for all his critics, be they conservative Hindu pandits or missionaries, through his prolific use of printed pamphlets and tracts. The print-induced "public" was redefined in most ways by Rammohun.[78] An instance of how theological disputes and discussions would have taken place in a pre-print age is evident in the formation and operation of the Atmiya Sabha. In 1815, Rammohun started the Atmiya Sabha, or Friendly Association, with a small group of friends. It met once a week, and its activities comprised chanting of hymns that were written by Rammohun and his friends, and the recitation of texts from the Hindu scriptures. Sivaprasad Misra, Rammohun's *pandit*, was the chief reciter. The meetings were not public; among the attendees can be mentioned Dwarkanath Tagore, Brajamohan Mazumdar, Haladhar Bose, Nandakisore Bose, and Rajnarayan Sen. Despite the institutional character of the Atmiya Sabha, it was a discursive space for debate, and is representative of the pre print and oral public spaces which functioned and allowed for theological debates.[79] Such kinds of socio-theological discussions were transferred onto print as a result of the emergence of a plethora of pamphlets and journals; Christian missionaries and Hindu orthodox *pandits* connected to the East India Company joined the fray.

Conservative Hindus were critical of Rammohun's brand of Hinduism. In December 1816, the *Madras Courier* carried a letter written by one Sankara Sastri, who was the head English teacher in Madras Government College. He was extremely critical of Rammohun's propagation of Hinduism. Rammohun replied to this letter in 1817 by publishing *A Defence of Hindoo Theism*[80] where he wrote:

> Before I attempt to reply to the observations that the learned gentlemen, who signs himself Sankara Sastri, has offered in his letter of the 26th December last, addressed to

---

[78] For a detailed analysis, see Collet, *Life and Letters*, pp. 69-209.

[79] See Ibid., pp. 432-441 regarding *The Trust Deed of the Brahmo Samaj*.

[80] *A Defence of Hindoo Theism. In Reply to the Attack of an Advocate for Idolatory in Madras. 1817.* In *The English Works of Raja Rammohun Roy. Part II*, pp. 83-93.

> the Editor of the *Madras Courier*, on the subject of an article published in the *Calcutta Gazette*, and on my translation of an abridgement of the Vedanta and of the two chapters of the Vedas, I beg to be allowed to express the disappointment I have felt in receiving from a learned Brahman controversial remarks on Hindoo Theology written in a foreign language, as it is the invariable practice of the natives of all provinces of Hindoostan to hold their discussions on such subjects in Sanskrit, which is the learned language common to all of them, and in which they may naturally be expected to convey their ideas with perfect correctness and greater facility than in any foreign tongue; nor need it be alleged that, by adopting this established channel of controversy, the opportunity of appealing to public opinion on the subject must be lost, as a subsequent translation from the Sanskrit into English may sufficiently serve that purpose.[81]

Rammohun displays surprise that English was the chosen medium for a theological debate between two learned *pandits* as Sanskrit was the accepted mode of discussion but he accepts the choice of language. English was often used by native intellectuals, and in the process, European readers were drawn into these theological debates. Mrityunjay Tarkalankar, the chief pandit connected to the College of Fort William and the finest scholar of Sanskrit in Bengal, also wrote against Rammohun in *Vedantachandrika*, which was subsequently translated into *An Apology for the Present System of Hindu Worship* in 1817. Rammohun's reply was *A Second Defence of The Monotheistical System of The Vedas In Reply to An Apology For the Present State of Hindoo Worship*[82] in 1817. He wrote:

> Two publications only have yet appeared with the professed object of defending Hindoo idolatry against the arguments which I have adduced from the Vedanta and other sacred authorities, in proof of the erroneousness of that system. To the first, which appeared in a Madras journal, my reply has been for some time before the public. The second, which is the object of the present

---

[81] Ibid., p. 83.

[82] *A Second Defence of The Monotheistical System of The Vedas In Reply to An Apology For the Present State of Hindoo Worship. 1817.* In *The English Works of Raja Rammohun Roy. Part II*, pp. 97-119.

answer, and is supposed to be the production of a learned Brahman now residing in Calcutta, was printed both in Bengali and in English; and I have therefore been under the necessity of preparing a reply in both of those languages. That which was intended for the perusal of my countrymen, issued from the press a few weeks ago. For my European readers I have thought it advisable to make some additional remarks to those contained in the Bengali publication, which I hope will tend to make my arguments more clear and intelligible to them than a bare translation would do.[83]

Rammohun distinguishes between his native readers, who were addressed differently from his English readers. Even those theological debates which were addressed to natives, as a result of the use of English printed texts soon included Europeans as readers. The realm of Hindu *pandits* using print was contiguous to the realm of English print being produced by the Britishers, and oftentimes English was used by the natives in order to include the Europeans in their theological debates.

The Brahmunical Magazine was another magazine that was started by Rammohun as a result of missionary attacks.[84] In the preface to the *Second Edition*, he wrote: "*The Brahmunical Magazine* was commenced for the purpose of answering the objections against the Hindoo Religion contained in a Bengalee Weekly Newspaper, entitled *Samachar Darpan*, conducted by some of the most eminent of the Christian missionaries, and published at Shreerampore."[85] He used print to engage with the missionaries and was quite vituperative in his attacks.[86] This is evident in his tract titled "A

---

[83] Ibid., p. 97.

[84] For a detailed analysis see, Collet, *Life and Letters*, pp. 118-171.

[85] "Preface to the Second Edition" of *The Brahmunical Magazine or The Missionary and the Brahmun*. Calcutta, 1821. In *The English Works of Raja Rammohun Roy. Part II*, p. 139.

[86] In the fourth volume of the *Brahmunical Magazine*, he wrote in 1823: "Notwithstanding my humble suggestions in the third number of this Magazine, against the use of offensive expressions in religious controversy, I find, to my great surprise and concern, in a small tract lately issued from one of the missionary presses and distributed by missionary gentlemen, direct charges of atheism made against the doctrines of the Vedas, and undeserved reflections on us as their followers. This has induced me to publish, after an interval of two years, a fourth number of the *Brahmunical Magazine*." In *The English Works of Raja Rammohun*

Dialogue Between a Missionary and Three Chinese Converts" which is extremely sarcastic in its tone, as the "missionary" in the text does not hesitate in describing Chinese Buddhism as emerging from the "devil."[87]

Rammohun took the efforts to learn Greek and Hebrew so that he could translate the Bible; in 1820, he published the *Precepts of Jesus* where he argued that his aim was to persuade his Christian readers to separate the miraculous from the "moral doctrines."[88] Affronted by the fact that a native wanted to preach the Bible to them, the missionaries described him as a heathen in *The Friend of India*, and this attack in turn offended Rammohun.[89] He replied to his charge by publishing *An Appeal to the Christian Public*. He wrote that the missionary method of promoting Christianity, was by "distributing in vain amongst the natives numberless copies of the Bible written in different languages."[90] He never "doubted their zeal" as "immense sums of money" was spent annually towards this. The "natives" refuse to believe in the "dogmas and mysteries taught in Christian Churches" and the Bible was received to be exchanged for "blank paper" and several of the "dogmatical terms" were used as a slight in "native language."[91] Such statements were, indeed, quite a slap in the face. Rammohun goes on to say: "I hope no one will infer that I feel ill disposed towards the Missionary establishments in this country. ... I pray for their augmentation and that their members may remain in the happy enjoyment of life in a climate so generally inimical to European constitution."[92] Enormous sarcasm is evident in these writings. Rammohun's relations with

---

Roy. Part II, p. 171.

[87] "A Dialogue Between a Missionary and Three Chinese Converts," In *The English Works of Raja Rammohun Roy. Part IV*, pp. 75-80.

[88] "Introduction" to *The Precepts of Jesus*. In *The English Works of Raja Rammohun Roy. Part V*, p. 4.

[89] In *An Appeal to the Christian Public*, Rammohun wrote: "... I humbly beg to appeal to the public against the unchristian like, as well as uncivil manner in which the Editor had adduced his objections to the compilation [of The Precepts of Jesus], by introducing personality, and applying the term heathen to the Compiler." In *The English Works of Raja Rammohun Roy. Part V*, p. 57.

[90] Collet, *Life and Letters*, p. 125.

[91] Ibid., pp. 125-126.

[92] Ibid., p.126.

the missionaries deteriorated; while *The Precepts* and the first two *Appeals* had been printed at the Baptist Missionary Press, the *Final Appeal* was printed at his own Unitarian Press at Dharamtala, Calcutta in 1823.[93] In this work, he was aware of his readership, and what was expected from him as a native writing on the Bible in English.

The world of British and native printers and editors was a small one and Rammohun's print endeavors were not in isolation. Native printers had to work in conjunction with British printers. Initially, Rammohun was helped by the missionary presses, but they parted ways after his publication of *The Precepts of Jesus*. Subsequently, he was helped by other editors. In 1821, an advertisement appeared in the *Calcutta Journal*, an English newspaper that was meant for the Europeans, which announced that a Bengali newspaper, owned by Rammohun, was to be printed by the natives and called *Sambad Kaumudi*, or the "The Moon of Intelligence": we "humbly solicit the support and patronage of all who feel themselves interested in the intellectual and moral improvement of our countrymen ... [who would contribute] to our paper a monthly subscription of two rupees."[94] The *Calcutta Journal* was owned by James Silk Buckingham, who was critical of certain governmental policies in his newspaper, and sympathetic to the native press, often publishing regular extracts from other native newspapers like the *Sambad Kaumudi* and *Mirat-ul-Akhbar*. Both of the latter were owned by Rammohun. After censorship was imposed in India, Buckingham was expelled in 1823.

Rammohun was keen to engage with European printers, but he was also willing to part ways if he faced criticism. His on and off relation with the Baptist missionaries is ample evidence. He cultivated relations that enabled him to learn the technology of print. He used his journals to address the native public on larger social issues. The first issue of the *Sambad Kaumudi* contained an "appeal to the government for the establishment of a School for the gratuitous instruction of the children of poor though respectable Hindus"; the second issue was an "address to the natives, enumerating the advantages of reading newspapers" and the third issue had an "appeal to the government to prevent the export of rice from Bengal to foreign ports [and also] an appeal to the government to enable

---

[93] Ibid., pp 118-171.

[94] Ibid., p. 173.

the middle class natives to have access to European doctors."[95] It is reductive to describe him as being the first to bring out newspapers that were used as an instrument to educate as he was preceded in his endeavors by the missionaries from whom he learnt and eventually retreated. The Srirampur Mission press can be credited with bringing out the first Bengali newspapers, or for that matter, bringing out printed journals that were meant for native readership. The publication of *Digdarsan*, in April 1818, which was printed monthly, was followed by the publication of another monthly publication called *The Friend of India*, in the same year, but in English. A weekly Bengali paper, *Samachar Darpan*, was also started in May 1818. Though Joshua Marshman was the editor, he was assisted in his work by two Hindu pandits, Jaygopal Tarkalankar and Tarinicharan Siromoni.[96] Thus, the realm of print involved both the natives and the Europeans.

Censorship

Print in the early years of the nineteenth century was in its formative stages and catered largely to the needs of the Europeans, which comprised officials attached to the East India company and independent traders and civilians who often opposed certain policies of the British government.[97] Many editors were critical of the ways in which the government operated. Inevitably, Lord Wellesley imposed censorship in India in 1799. All editors, printers and proprietors of newspapers had to register with the government and all material that was meant for publication was to be submitted in advance to the government for inspection. Violation of these rules meant deportation to England. The offenders were primarily English. Censorship was relaxed after the departure of Wellesley in 1805, and was completely removed in 1818 by Lord Hastings. Though native presses were not affected, Rammohun, as a result of his intimacy with the European printers, shared their concerns against censorship, coming out with a *Petition against the Press Regulation* in 1823,[98] where he earnestly argued against the need for

---

[95] Ibid., p.173.

[96] The government requested the Mission Press to bring out Persian publications of the newspaper, in order to reach across to the people of upper India, and accordingly in 1826, the *Akhbare Srirampur* was printed. It ceased publication after a few months due to lack of patronage.

[97] Sivnath Sastri, *Ramtanu Lahiri*, p. 161. He argues that many English editors were against the manner in which the fourth Mysore War was fought by the British army.

[98] *Petitions against the Press Regulations*. In *The English Works of Raja Rammohun Roy. Part IV*, pp. 1-9.

censorship. Moreover, his response was immediate and enormous as he withdrew publication of his Persian journal *Mirat-ul-Akhbar*. The Petition was also signed by five other natives—Chandra Kumar Thakur, Dwarkanath Tagore, Harchandra Ghosh, Gauricharan Bannerjee, Prasanna Kumar Thakur. It is not known whether this group of the native elite was directly involved in the realm of print culture in the manner as Rammohun was. Therefore, we are unable to figure out the rationale behind the element of earnestness and self-righteousness that is revealed in the "Petition" though we do get a glimpse of the nature of native reading and the writing public. Reading Rammohun's petition, one arrives at the conclusion that there was a plethora of native publishing, but the reality was far from this. A report by Bentinck[99] regarding the use of newspapers by natives reveals some interesting facts about native readership: ten English newspapers were circulated out of Calcutta; moreover, native newspapers were a "luxury" beyond Calcutta.[100] Within Calcutta, there were "rich and enlightened natives" but they were "few in number" and had little "influence" upon the population, and were "incapable of political mischief."[101] Actually, Indians had barely started to use print.

Rammohun was a cultural intermediary, bridging the gap between the natives, the missionaries, and the government. In *The Petition*, Rammohun was addressing the non-native public. *The Petition* is quite grandiose, and Rammohun begins by citing the implicit trust that the natives had placed in the Britishers, drawing upon the notion of the social contract of good governance that should exist between the rulers and the ruled: "Your Lordship is well aware that the Natives of Calcutta and its vicinity, have voluntarily entrusted Government with millions of their wealth, without indicating the least suspicion of its stability and good faith ... [with the hope] their interests will be as permanent as the British Power itself; while on the contrary, their fathers were invariably compelled to conceal their treasures in the bowels of the earth, in order to preserve them from the insatiable rapacity of their oppressive Rulers."[102] He goes on to elaborate as

---

[99] "Bentinck's minute on the Press dated January 6, 1829" In *The correspondences of Lord William Cavendish*, Vol. I. ed. C.H. Philips (1977), p. 136.

[100] Ibid., p. 138.

[101] Ibid., p. 139

[102] *Petitions against the Press Regulations*, p. 4.

to why the native population was in favor of the British government, stating that "the constant and the familiar topic of discourse among the Hindu community of Bengal" was "the literary and political improvements which are continually going on in the state of the country under the present system of Government, and a comparison between their present auspicious prospects and their hopeless condition under their former Rulers."[103] This notion of the glorious present and the oppressive past is a recurrent one in many of his writings, and is very specific to English historiography and its invention of the Indian past. In fact, Rammohun's personal history where his family had been intrinsically involved with the Muslims is elided.

The Indians, Rammohun argues, want the protection of the British, and have "voluntarily" come forward to support the British in all respects. The British have *reciprocated* by establishing schools and institutions of higher learning. Moreover, he writes:

> [E]ver since the art of printing has become generally known among the Natives of Calcutta, numerous Publications have been circulated in the Bengalee Language, which by introducing free discussion among the Natives and inducing them to reflect and inquire after knowledge, have already served greatly to improve their minds and ameliorate their condition. This desirable object has been chiefly promoted by the establishment of four Native newspapers ...[104]

The English newspapers were causing dissent but not the native ones. He argues that the Government would encourage the establishment of more newspapers which would inform the government as to what was taking place in different parts of the country, but instead the government had imposed severe restrictions.[105]

Censorship would put a complete stop "to the diffusion of knowledge and the consequent mental improvement now going on, either by translations into the popular dialect of this country from the learned languages of the East, or by the circulation of literary intelligence drawn

---

[103] Ibid., p. 5

[104] Ibid., p. 6.

[105] Ibid., p. 6-7

from foreign publications."[106] Most importantly, it would stop communication between the natives and the English rulers. He writes, censorship would

> preclude the Natives from communicating frankly and honestly to their Gracious Sovereign in England and his Council, the real conditions of his Majesty's faithful subjects in this distant part of his dominions ... : since such information cannot in future be conveyed to England, as it has heretofore been, either by the translations from the Native publications inserted in the English newspapers printed here and sent to Europe, or by the English publications which the Natives themselves had in contemplation to establish, ...[107]

Rammohun did make an epistemic shift in terms of being able to learn the etiquette of print, and in addressing a non native readership; he was able to step outside his own socio-racial identity and refer to himself in the third person, describing natives in terms that were comprehensible to his readers. What is also of interest is the fact that Rammohun was imagining a native readership that was absent, but would inevitably emerge with time. Native readers and their involvement with print culture would increase, according to Rammohun, as a result of interaction with the Britishers, and as a result of governmental policies.

Conclusion

Here, I have looked at the broader canvas of how natives were involved in the imperial realm of print as compositors, writers, booksellers, printers, teachers and translators, mastering and replicating all aspects of print culture and technology. My specific focus has been on Rammohun Roy's engagement with this emerging realm of print, thus tracing the transition that took place from imperial print to native print. This process of cultural transmission and exchange did not pass through any phase of mimicry. In fact, the natives learnt about print and used it in a manner which cannot be contained with the notion of mimicry. There was close intimacy between the Britishers and the natives; an intimacy that did not operate on dislike,

---

[106] Ibid., p. 7

[107] Ibid., p. 7

oppression or contempt.

Conclusion.

a) Exchange through close intimacy.

When we trace the minute details of how native print entrepreneurs learnt from European printers, we can understand how the transfer of technology had taken place -- for example, a printer of an established English newspaper would hire about 80 to 100 compositors[108]; mostly "Portuguese of the country" and "Hindoos."[109] The Hindoo compositors could not read English at all but acquired surprising expertness in their work, and gradually outnumbered the Portuguese. As late as 1846, one James Hume, the proprietor of the *Calcutta Star* commented on their inability to read English and how it was a disadvantage as they made a "sorry work of manuscript copy."[110] Nonetheless, natives picked up expertise in establishing their own realm of the communication circuit.

The early years of the nineteenth century saw the emergence of numerous native-owned publishing ventures, which were modeled on the British establishments and run by Indians who had worked in some capacity with the first British-owned printing presses in Calcutta, but mostly catered to the native readers.[111] Gangakishore Bhattacharya's Bangal Gajeti Press, which was the first Bengali press owned by natives, was formed around 1818, and as he was also a publisher, he started a Bengali weekly called the *Bangal Gajeti*. His career as a printer reveals the process of cultural and technological exchange that had taken place. Bhattacharya had been an employee of the Srirampur Mission Press, working as a compositor. He left the press and published some works at Ferris and Company in Calcutta, the most notable text being the 18th century poet, Bharatchandra's *Annadamangal Kabya* in 1816. The success of these printed works made him open an office and a bookshop; eventually he started the Bangal Gajeti Press. One of the co-owners of this press was Harachandra Roy, who was also a member of Rammohun Roy's Atmiya Sabha. Rammohun would have

---

[108] *Bengal Harkaru*, 24 May 24th (1825).

[109] "Reply to Question No.1130 of the Examination of James Sutherland on March 16, 1832," *Parliamentary Paper*, House of Commons, 1831-32, Vol. 9, Paper 735, I, p. 126.

[110] *Calcutta Star*, 26 December (1846).

[111] See Abu Henā Mostaphā Kāmāla, *The Bengali Press and Literary Writing, 1818-31*, 1st edition. (Dacca: University Press, 1977).

known Harachandra Roy, which explains how he was well informed about the activities of the printing community in Calcutta; it also explains why Rammohun was able to quickly have his treatises and polemical tracts printed.

b) A new work space: Britishers and *pandits*.

There was no clear cut boundary between teacher and the taught in the new realm of print that emerged – the Englishmen learnt native languages and customs from the Indians, while the latter were introduced to all the new facets of print. William Carey (1761-1834), a Baptist missionary, was a pioneer of sorts in his efforts to print a large number of texts in Bengali. His teacher, Ramram Bose, helped him with the translations. In order to print it, Bengali fonts were needed, and Carey was assisted by Panchanan Karmakar in setting up a printing press in Malda. Carey, along with the other missionaries, formed the Baptist Mission in 1800 and in order to make a functional printing press, was joined by Karmakar in the same year. Karmakar was assisted by another craftsman and a pupil of Charles Wilkins, Manohar Karmakar. The Baptist Mission Press worked closely with *pandits*, who also printed books of fiction in Bengali – they were the first writers in Bengali who had their works printed. Rammohun Roy was familiar with this group of writers, and undoubtedly would have learned the processes that were involved in writing books for printing houses.

c) Returning the gaze of mimicry.

It is not an exaggeration to say that Rammohun was the first native to understand what it meant to participate in the newly established print communication circuit – by engaging with printers, and starting his own printing house and mastering the English language and the technology of print culture. As a writer, Rammohun was able to imagine the needs of his readers, and adroitly negotiate between his English readers and his native readers. Rammohun had a readership that was immense in its diversity for that time period.[112] It would be extremely myopic of us to estimate that

---

[112] His books found their way into the hands of Jeremy Bentham, who, in a letter described him as "Intensely Admired and Dearly Beloved Collaborator in the Service of Mankind." (Letter by Jeremy Bentham to Rammohun Roy," in Collet, *Life and Letters*, pp. 452). The *Precepts of Jesus* found its way to England, and it inspired the Earl of Northbrook to publish his *The Teachings of Jesus Christ in His Own Words*. (Published by *Sampson Low*. London, 1990). In the preface, the Earl wrote: "My purpose has been to put before them [the People of India] the Teaching of Christ in His Own words, as recorded in the four Gospels … The learned and distinguished Hindu, Raja Rammohun Roy, published eighty years ago a compilation called

Rammohun Roy was a passive recipient of this new culture and technology that was being set up in Calcutta. He was situated at the cusp of those very changes, and even as he picked up the socio-cultural processes of print culture, he used it to negotiate against the bullying tactics of many of the missionaries and conservative Christians who seemed to have found their way to India. Rammohun categorized the manner in which proselytisation took place: books were published and distributed amongst the natives reviling the Hindu gods; the second method involved "standing in front of the doors of the natives or in the public roads" to preach the greatness of Christianity and the "debasedness" of the others; and the third was to convert low caste people and hold them as examples for other natives to follow.[113] This exchange of religious opinion was not a passive exercise, whereby the missionaries coerced the natives to accept Christianity, but in fact, involved a great deal of humouring and satirising on the part of the natives. When Rammohun's *Precepts of Jesus* received enormous negative commentaries from an English reader, Dr Tytler in the *Bengal Harkaru*, who was a surgeon in the East India Company, and also a member of the Asiatic Society, Rammohun retaliated in the form of letters by assuming the name of Ram Doss, an orthodox Hindu and an opponent of all tenets of Unitarianism. Ram Doss pretended to be an enemy of Rammohun. This correspondence was published in a pamphlet titled: "A Vindication of the Incarnation of Deity as the common basis of Hinduism and Christianity against the schismatic Attacks of R. Tytler"[114] by Rammohun himself. The supposedly civilizing gaze of the Britishers was mocked by Rammohun, who could through his command of English and print, turn around the very means that were used to critique him.

The Precepts of Jesus (p. v).

[113] "Preface to the First Edition" of *The Brahmunical Magazine*, Calcutta, 1821. In *The English Works of Raja Rammohun Roy. Part II*, p. 137.

[114] "A Vindication of the Incarnation of Deity as the common basis of Hinduism and Christianity against the schismatic Attacks of R. Tytler." In *The English Works of Raja Rammohun Roy. Part IV*, pp. 56-74.

4 CONCLUSION

Intimacy and enmity between printers and writers, Britishers and natives.

It was an extremely small realm of print, where Englishmen and natives involved in the production of knowledge, and in the technology of print, knew each other. The same metallurgists and printers were involved in different printing houses. For example, Bengali letterpress technology was transferred from the East India Company to the Baptist Mission Press. Everyone involved in the trade seemed to know each other. The terrain of print was also a contested one. Many of the writers and printers began as friends but turned rivals, parting ways when ideological differences arose. If we look at some of the seminal works of Rammohun Roy and how they were printed, and under what circumstances, we understand the nature of this terrain. The Baptist Missionary Press published texts that proselytized for Christianity and also printed Rammohun's works that were critical of Christianity. Rammohun was closely attached to the Baptist missionaries, and many of his works on Christianity were printed there. But the Baptist missionaries were not happy with him. This was a bit of a sticky situation as the Baptist Mission press was his publishing house for all the works on the subject of Christianity. Eventually, they refused to publish his works, and in 1823, he printed *The Final Appeal to the Christian Public in Defence of the Precepts of Jesus* which was printed at the Unitarian Press—Rammohun had had to buy his own type and rely on native superintendence.

Debates were made possible through print and they also spilled into the realm of native intellectuals and theologians. Rammohun positioned himself against many of the existing well known *pandits* who were associated with British establishments. Many Indian *pandits*, attached with the Baptist Mission Press, also printed books in Bengali that were of a fictional nature. For example, *Batris Simhasan* was published by Mrityunjar Tarkalankar in 1802. But more importantly, Rammohun was involved in theological debate with Mrityunjay Vidyalankar, who was also the head *pandit* of the government college at Calcutta around 1817. Mrityunjay's

Vedanta Chandrika (translated into English as *An Apology for the Present System of Hindu Worship*) was critiqued by Rammohun in A *Second Defense of the Monotheistical System of the Veds* (*Bhattacharyer Sahit Vichar*). In this realm of print, Rammohun engaged in debate with certain brands of Christianity and Hinduism. There was a blurry line between enemies and friends.

New theoretical interventions.

A hazy picture of the early years of print and intellectual engagement emerges as I conclude my book. Hindu natives rubbing shoulders with the Europeans; the new establishment of a city with all the paraphernalia of European civilization—many natives were going to eventually be "suited" and "booted." Ships arrived at the docks loaded with books, consumer items for the colonizers, and a whole lot of material for printing presses; it also came loaded with men who brought intellectual labour. Alongside Hindu and Islamic cultures, a new civilization emerged in India. How do we account for this degree of pluralism and multi-culturalism? I am immediately drawn to Paul Gilroy's theoretical position in *The Black Atlantic as a Counterculture of Modernity*, where he argues against nationalist or ethnically absolute identities, specifically the English nation state which defines itself as "ceaselessly" giving birth to itself, "seemingly from Britannia's head."[115] Gilroy draws attention to the possibility of a transnational and transcultural perspective—the Atlantic, which gave birth to the black diaspora, can affect how we view the western hemisphere, and concepts of ethnic authenticity. As Gilroy argues, one needs double consciousness in order to be both "European and black,"[116] like the numerous travelers and exiles like William Du Bois, Richard Wright and Martin Robison Delaney. Ships moving between nations, "crossing borders in modern machines" were "micro systems of linguistic and political hybridity."[117] The western artistic imagination of the eighteenth century was replete with icons of the ship, or the slave ship; "ships were the living means by which the points within that Atlantic world were joined."[118]

News of sailing ships was an important and regular feature in the Indian newspapers that were printed in the last two decades of the

---

[115] Paul Gilroy, *The Black Atlantic: Modernity and Double Consciousness* (London, Verso, 1993), p.14.

[116] Ibid., p. 1.

[117] Ibid., p. 12.

[118] Ibid., p. 16.

eighteenth century. Ships were the most important links between the colonies and the metropole; Most importantly, ships carried more than goods and news—they carried people who started British establishments that were more than trading enclaves in different parts of India. Thereby, the whole of Indian society underwent gradual changes, adding a European identity to the existing Islamic and Hindu ones. Such a perspective allows us to look at the processes of colonialism from a global angle. This area of studies is in its nascent stages and a lot more work could be done on the "double consciousness" of Rammohun Roy, and the initial realms of English print.

I consider "double consciousness" to be definitive of a lot of English writings emerging from India and is also evident in the first generation of native writers who wrote novels in the vernacular in the nineteenth century, Bankimchandra Chattopadhay and Michael Madhusudan Dutta, while they both continued to write their personal correspondence in English.[119] Meenakshi Mukherjee writes that this kind of bilingualism is also present in the writings of Govardhanram Tripathi, who wrote a novel, *Saraswatichandra,* in Gujrati while his extensive personal entries were in English. While *Saraswatichandra* appeared in four volumes between 1887 and 1900, his introspective personal English prose of this time period was of 1200 manuscript pages. It was as if the most natural act was to write a diary in English and a novel in Gujrati simultaneously.[120] This "complexity in the linguistic circumstances" is evident is that these writers use English in their personal interaction with friends, while the "artifact shaped for public consumption" was in an Indian language; at this moment in time, for natives, English was not the preferred language for "literary recognition either regionally or nationally."[121] The notion of "double consciousness" as a term can be used to explain how native writers in English inhabited multiple socio-cultural linguistic spaces.

Further Implications: Transference of Modernity through print.

I conclude my book by referring to a letter that Jeremy Bentham wrote to

---

[119] Meenakshi Mukerjee, *The Perishable Empire. Essays on Indian Writing in English* (New Delhi: Oxford University Press, 2002), p. 9.

[120] Ibid., p. 10.

[121] Ibid., pp. 10-11.

Rammohun in 1831,[122] where Bentham describes himself as having had a great influence on James Mill who dictated the histories of India through his work, *The History of British India* (1818); Mill is seen as a family friend, a discipline and a student of Bentham. What is of immense interest is how Bentham subtly suggests to Rammohun that his ideas have been influential in determining the future of India, via the various people whom he knew (he mentions many officials of the EIC and James Mill, of course) and therefore, his establishment of the new penal system in England—the panopticon—is also an institution that Rammohun could consider for India. Bentham wrote, requesting Rammohun to join in the process of establishing an ideal prison system in India:

> What say you to the making singly or in conjunction with other enlightened philanthropists, an offer to Government for that purpose [of building the panopticon]? Professors of all religion might join the contract; and appropriate classification and separation for the persons under management provision correspondent to their several religions, and their respective castes; or other allocations under their respective religions.[123]

This is a fascinating anecdote to narrate, showing us the near macabre ways in which the new modern systems of knowledge that were emerging in the West were transferred to the colonies; Bentham suggests that the bodies of the native inmates would be classified and separated according to their religions and castes and a new panoptical system could be established in India. According to Michel Foucault, the panopticon's method of classifying and codifying was a perfect example of the new forms of knowledge systems that emerged in the eighteenth and nineteenth centuries where knowledge was intrinsically connected with power.[124] Foucault describes how the eighteenth- to nineteenth-century transformation of the human sciences was "set in the context of practices of discipline, surveillance, and constraint, which made possible new kinds of knowledge

---

[122] Letter from Jeremy Bentham to Rammohun Roy" in Sophia Dobson Collet, *The Life and Letters of Raja Rammohun Roy*, ed. Dilip Kumar Biswas and Prabhat Chandra Ganguli. (Calcutta: Sadharon Brahmo Samaj, 1900). Reprint 1988, pp.452-456.

[123] Ibid., p. 456.

[124] Michel Foucault, *Discipline and Punishment. The Birth of a Prison.* (New York: Vintage, 1995). Also see Michel Foucault, *The History of Sexuality, Vol. I*.(New York: Vintage, 1990).

of human beings even as they created new forms of social control."[125] The new systems of human sciences allowed for greater knowledge about the self, but simultaneously, made it inevitable that the body would be under greater control. State sponsored surveillance and discipline of the body produced "docile" bodies; as Foucault wrote:

> The human body was entering a machinery of power that explores it, breaks it down and rearranges it. . . . It defined how one may have a hold over others' bodies, not only so that they may do what one wishes, but so that they may operate as one wishes, with the techniques, the speed and the efficiency that one determines. Thus discipline produces subjected and practiced bodies, "docile" bodies.[126]

Bentham's prison system was one such institution which, through its method of control and surveillance of the inmates, was meant to create reformed bodies. The letter that Bentham wrote to Rammohun indicates that the structural changes that were taking place in the eighteenth and the nineteenth centuries, were in the process of being transferred to the colonies. In the colonies, though, the very nature of colonial power itself underwent transformation; the book had the power to change the native social structures. The natives took print culture and used it for their means. The transference of western modernity through these figures and print is a subject that needs to be examined at further lengths.

What needs to be done? For the future of book history in India.

i. Scholarship on print culture in its early years.

We in the present write, speak, imagine and function in English. Where did it all begin and how did it begin? This is a story that is not yet told. Barely two hundred years have passed, and we have claimed legitimacy for a language that is not indigenous to India. There are many native figures that crop us as we go through some of the histories of the early decades of the nineteenth century; for example, I am sure much can be written about the various editors of Rammohun Roy's Bengali newspaper, *Sambad Kaumudi*

---

[125] Joseph Rouse, "Power and Knowledge," in *The Cambridge Companion to Foucault*, ed. Gary Gutting (Cambridge: Cambridge University Press, 2006), pp. 95-122.

[126] Michel Foucault, *Discipline and Punishment*, p. 138.

(1821)—Bhabanicharan Bandhopadhay, Harihar Datta, and Gobindachandra Konar; who were they? Many other entrepreneurs set up native newspapers. In 1823, Krishnomohan Das was granted a license to bring out a newspaper called *Sambad Timiranasak*. It was intended to support the doctrines of Hinduism, and positioned itself against newspapers like *Sambad Kaumudi* and *Samachar Darpan*. Post censorship, in 1829, one Robert Montgomery Martin was given permission to print a journal called the *Bengal Herald* in four languages; the *Bengal Herald* was in English, and *Bangadut* was in Bengali, Persian and Nagree. *Bangadut* was owned and financed by R.M. Martin, Dwarkanath Thakur, Rammohun Roy and Prasannakumar Thakur, and the journal was edited by Nilratan Haldar. Within a few months time, though, a few of the patrons withdrew financial support. Interestingly enough, satirical works made their appearance in the *Samachar Darpan* in 1821; two prose works were published by the title of *Babur Upakhyan (The Story of a Babu)*. The author was seen as Bhabanicharan Bandhopadhay, who also published a few other works—*Naba Babu Bilas*, *Duti Bilas* and *Naba Bibi Bilas* - around the 1820s. There is scant knowledge of these various journals and people who dotted the domain of print in the early decades of the nineteenth century.

A lot of more work can be done by looking at the newspapers of the late eighteenth and early centuries. I would also hope that a library-cum-museum of sorts can be opened which would house these journals and newspapers. Easy access to these primary texts will encourage more scholarship.

ii. Translation Studies.

For those of us situated in the interstices of cultural and literary studies, it would be very relevant to have access to the nearly forgotten texts that I have mentioned above. Translations of such Bengali works into English would add much to our knowledge of the early years of print.

iii. Emergence of new disciplines.

New disciplines can emerge, which are situated at the juncture of literary, cultural and textual studies and would involve knowledge of both English and Indian writings. Such a field cannot be slighted off as something like South-east Asian studies. Moreover, for us in India, where we have access to primary texts in specific areas, it makes sense to focus on what we have. A resource like the National Library in Kolkata is a prime example of an underused institution as it is a repository of a great many texts that are not readily available in other parts of the world. We can initiate disciplinary changes within literary studies by making use of the primary texts that are easy to obtain, and unique to our social location. Scholarship that emerges from such a space becomes cutting edge and original. The nature of the discipline itself can undergo change and more emphasis can be given on reading archival material. We can, therefore, change the very nature of how literary studies is done in India, and question the tenuous and hierarchical relationship between English and Indian languages.

Conclusion.

I have examined here but one slice of the numerous encounters that took place between the colonizers and the colonized. Looking at the historical specificities of these engagements allow us to understand that it was a process that was quite complex. The book was not exactly an act of mimicry; neither can it be described as a hybrid text. In many ways, the book was the result of the inevitable flow of time, and the interaction of cultures.

APPENDICES.

APPENDIX A. AUTOBIOGRAPHICAL SKETCH[127]

MY DEAR FRIEND,

In conformity with the wish, you have frequently expressed, that I should give you an outline of my life, I have now the pleasure to give you the following very brief sketch.

My ancestors were Brahmins of a high order, and, from time immemorial, were devoted to the religious duties of their race, down to my fifth progenitor, who about one hundred and forty years ago gave up spiritual exercises for worldly pursuits and aggrandisement. His descendants ever since have followed his example, and, according to the usual fate of courtiers, with various success, sometimes rising to honour and sometimes falling; sometimes rich and sometimes poor; sometimes excelling in success, sometimes miserable through disappointment. But my maternal ancestors, being of the sacerdotal order by profession as well as by birth, and of a family than which none holds a higher
rank in that profession, have up to the present day uniformly adhered to a life of religious observances and devotion, preferring peace and tranquility of mind to the excitements of ambition, and all the allurements of worldly grandeur.

---

[127] Miss Carpenter thus introduced this Autobiographical Sketch into her book, *Last days in England of Raja Ram Mohon Roy* : "The letter from Rammohon Roy himself first appeared in the *Atheneum*, and in the *Literary Gazette*, from one or other of which it was copied into various newspapers. It was written just before he went to France. It was probably designed for some distinguished person who had desired him to give an out line of his history; and he adopted this form for the purpose. The letter may be considered as addressed to his friend Mr. Gordon, of Calcutta."

In conformity with the usage of my paternal race, and the wish of my father, I studied the Persian and Arabic languages, these being indispensable to those who attached themselves to the courts of the Mahommedan princes; and agreeably to the usage of my maternal relations, I devoted myself to the study of the Sanskrit and the theological works written in it, which contain the body of Hindoo literature, law and religion.
When about the age of sixteen, I composed a manuscript calling in question the validity of the idolatrous system of the Hindoos. This, together with my known sentiments on that subject, having produced a coolness between me and my immediate kindred, I proceeded on my travels, and passed through different countries, chiefly within, but some beyond, the bounds of Hindoostan, with a feeling of great aversion to the establishment of the British power in India. When I had reached the age of twenty, my father recalled me, and restored me to his favour; after which I first saw and began to associate with Europeans, and soon after made myself tolerably acquainted with their laws and form of government. Finding them generally more intelligent, more steady and moderate in their conduct, I gave up my prejudice against them, and became inclined in their favour, feeling persuaded that their rule, though a foreign yoke, would lead more speedily and surely to the amelioration of the native inhabitants; and I enjoyed the confidence of several of them even in their public capacity. My continued controversies with the Brahmins on the subject of their idolatry and superstition, and my interference with their custom of burning widows, and other pernicious practices, reviled and increased their animosity against me; and through their influence with my family, my father was again obliged to withdraw his countenance openly, though his limited pecuniary support was still continued to me.

After my father's death I opposed the advocates of idolatry with still greater boldness. Availing myself of the art of printing, now established in India, I published various works and pamphlets against their errors, in the native and foreign languages. This raised such a feeling against me, that I was at last deserted by every person except two or three Scotch friends, to whom, and the nation to which they belong, I always feel grateful.

The ground which I took in all my controversies was, not that of opposition to Brahmmism but to a perversion of it; and I endeavoured to show that the idolatry of the Brahmins was contrary to the practice of their ancestors, and the principles of the ancient books and authorities which they profess to revere and obey. Not withstanding the violence of the opposition and resistance to my opinions, several highly respectable persons, both among my own relation and others, began to adopt the same sentiments.

I now felt a strong wish to visit Europe, and obtain by personal observation, a more thorough insight into its manners, customs, religion, and political institution. I refrained, however, from carrying this intention into effect until the friends who coincided in my sentiments should be increased in number and strength. My expectations having been at length realized, in November, 1830, I embarked for England, as the discussion of the East India Company's charter was expected to come on, by which the treatment of the natives of India, and its future government, would be determined for many years to come, and an appeal to the King in Council, against the abolition of the practice of burning widows, was to be heard before the Privy Council; and his Majesty the Emperor of Delhi had likewise commissioned me to bring before the authorities in England certain encrochments on his rights by the East India Company. I accordingly arrived in England in April, 1831.

I hope you will excuse the brevity of this sketch, as I have no leisure at present to enter into particulars, and
I remain,

RAMMOHUN ROY.

APPENDIX B: *THE BRAHMUNICAL MAGAZINE OR THE MISSIONARY AND THE BRAHMUN BEING A VINDICATION OF THE HINDOO RELIGION AGAINST THE ATTACKS OF CHRISTIAN MISSIONARIES.*
CALCUTTA,
1821.

PREFACE TO THE FIRST EDITION.

For a period of upwards of fifty years, this country (Bengal) has been in exclusive possession of the English nation; during the first thirty years of which, from their word and deed, it was universally believed that they would not interfere with the religion of their subjects, and that they truly wished every man to act in such matters according to the dictates of his own conscience. Their possessions in Hindoostan and their political strength have, through the grace of God gradually increased. But during the last twenty years, a body of English gentlemen who are called missionaries, have been publicly endeavouring, in several ways, to convert Hindoos and Mussulmans of this country into Christianity. The first way is that of publishing and distributing among the natives various books, large and small, reviling both religions, and abusing and ridiculing the gods and saints of the former: the second way is that of standing in front of the doors of the natives or in the public roads to preach the excellency of their own religion and the debasedness of that of others: the third way is that if any natives of low origin become Christians from the desire of gain or from any other motives, these gentlemen employ and maintain them as a necessary encouragement to others to follow their example.

It is true that the apostles of Jesus Christ used to preach the superiority of the Christian religion to the natives of different countries. But we must recollect that they were not of the rulers of those countries where they preached. Were the missionaries likewise to preach the Gospel and distribute books in countries not conquered by the English, such as Turkey, Persia, &c., which are such nearer England, they would be esteemed a body of men truly zealous in propagating their religion and in following the example of the founders of Christianity. In Bengal, where the English are the sole rulers, and where the mere name of Englishman is sufficient to frighten people, an encroachment upon the rights of her poor timid and humble inhabitants and upon their religion, cannot be viewed in the eyes of God or the public as a justifiable act. For wise and good men always feel disinclined to hurt those that are of much less strength than themselves, and if such weak creatures be dependent on them and subject to their authority, they can never attempt, even in thought, to mortify their feelings.

We have been subjected to such insults for about nine centuries, and the cause of such degradation has been our excess in civilization and abstinence from the slaughter even of animals; as well as our division into castes, which has been the source of want of unity
among us.

It seems almost natural that when one nation succeeds in conquering another, the former, though their religion may be quite ridiculous, laugh at and despise the religion and manners of those that are fallen into their power. For example, Mussulmans, upon their conquest of India, proved highly inimical to the religious exercises of Hindoos. When the generals of Chungezkhan, who denied God and were like wild beasts in their manners, invaded the western part of Hindoostan, they universally mocked at the profession of God and of futurity expressed to them by the natives of India. The savages of Arracan, on their invasion of the eastern part of Bengal, always attempted to degrade the religion of Hindoos. In ancient days, the Greeks and the Romans, who were gross idolators and immoral in their lives, used to laugh at the religion and conduct of their Jewish subjects, a sect who were devoted to the belief of one God. It is therefore not uncommon if the English missionaries, who are of the conquerors of this country, revile and mock at the religion of its natives. But as the English are celebrated for the manifestation of humanity and for administering justice, and as a great many gentlemen among them are noticed to have had an aversion to violate equity, it would tend to destroy their acknowledged character if they follow the example of the former savage conquerors in disturbing the established religion of the country; because to introduce a religion by means of abuse and insult, or by affording the hope of worldly gain, is inconsistent with reason and justice. If by the force of argument they can prove the truth of their own religion and the falsity of that of Hindoos, many would of course embrace their doctrines, and in case they fail to prove this, they should not undergo such useless trouble, nor tease Hindoos any longer by their attempts at conversion. In consideration of the small huts in which Brahmuns of learning generally reside, and the simple food, such as vegetables &c., which they are accustomed to eat, and the poverty which obliges them to live upon charity, the missionary gentlemen may not, I hope, abstain from controversy from contempt of them,
for truth and true religion do not always belong to -wealth and power, high names, or lofty palaces.

Now, in the Mission-press of Shreerampore a letter showing the unreasonableness of all the Hindoo Shastrus having appeared, I have inserted in the 1st and 2nd number of this magazine all the questions in the above letter as well as their answers, and afterwards the replies that may be made by both parties shall in like manner be published.

PREFACE TO THE SECOND EDITION.

In giving the contents of the following pages to the world in a new edition, I think it necessary to prefix a short explanation of the origin of the controversy, and the manner in which it concluded. The BRAHMUNICAL MAGAZINE was commenced for the purpose of answering the objections against the Hindoo Religion contained in a Bengallee Weekly Newspaper, entitled "SUMMACHAR DURPUN," conducted by some of the most eminent of the Christian Missionaries, and published at Shreerampore. In that paper of the 14th July, 1821, a letter was inserted containing certain doubts regarding the Shastrus, to which the writer invited any one to favour him with an answer, through the same channel. I accordingly sent a reply in the Bengallee language, to which, however, the conductors of the work calling for it, refused insertion; and I therefore formed the resolution of publishing the whole controversy with an English translation in a work of my own "the Brahmunical Magazine," now re-printed, which contains all that was written on both sides.

In the first number of the MAGAZINE I replied to the arguments they adduced against the Shastrus, or immediate explanations of the Veds, our original Sacred Books; and in the second I answered the objections urged against the Poorans and Tantras, or Historical Illustrations of the Hindoo Mythology, showing that the doctrines of the former are much more rational than the religion which the Missionaries profess, and that those of the latter, if unreasonable, are not more so than their Christian Faith. To this the Missionaries made a reply in their work entitled the "FRIEND OF INDIA," No. 38, which was immediately answered by me in the 3rd No. of the Magazine; and from the continuation of a regular controversy of this kind, I expected that in a very short time, the truth or fallacy of one or other of our religious systems would be clearly established; but to my great surprise and disappointment, the Christian Missionaries, after having provoked the discussion, suddenly abandoned it; and the 3rd No. of my Magazine has remained unanswered for nearly two years. During that long period the Hindoo community, (to whom the work was particularly addressed and therefore printed both in Bengallee and English), have made up their minds that the arguments of the BRAHMUNICAL MAGAZINE are unanswerable; and I now republish, therefore, only the English translation, that the learned among Christians, in Europe as well as in Asia, may form their opinion on the subject.

It is well-known to the whole world, that no people on earth are more tolerant than the Hindoos, who believe all men to be equally within the reach of Divine beneficence, which embraces the good of every religious sect and denomination: therefore it cannot be imagined that my object in publishing this Magazine was to oppose Christianity; but I was influenced by the conviction that persons who travel to a distant country for the purpose of overturning the opinions of its inhabitants and introducing their own, ought to be prepared to demonstrate that the latter are more reasonable than the former.

In conclusion, I beg to ask every candid and reflecting reader: Whether a man be placed on an imperial throne, or sit in the dust whether he be lord of the whole known world, or destitute of even a hut the commander of millions, or without a single follower whether he be intimately acquainted with all human learning, or ignorant of letters whether he be ruddy and handsome, or dark and deformed yet if while he declares that God is not man, he again professes to believe in a God-Man or Man-God, under whatever sophistry the idea may be sheltered, can such a person have a just claim to enjoy respect in the intellectual world? and does he not expose himself to censure, should he, at the same time, ascribe unreasonableness to others ?

APPENDIX C: A VINDICATION OF THE INCARNATION OF THE DEITY.[128]

DEDICATION.
TO ALL BELIEVERS IN THE INCARNATION OF THE DEITY.

Fellow Believers,

The following Correspondence between the Renowned Dr. B. Tytler and my self, was partly given to the world through the medium of the *Bengal Harkaru*, but as the Editor of that Paper refused to admit some of my letters into its pages, and those published were widely separated from each other by being mixed up with various extraneous matters, I have deemed it advisable to have the whole collected together and presented at one view, for general edification.

My object in addressing Dr. Tytler (as will be seen from a perusal of the following pages,) was, that all Believers in the Manifestation of God in the flesh, whether Hindoo or Christian, might unite in support of our Common Cause, and cordially co-operate in our endeavours to check the alarming growth of the Unitarian Heresy: but unfortunately my hopes were entirely disappointed; as Dr. Tytler not only refused to repair the breach 1 conceived his writings calculated to make, but to my great surprise and regret, in return for my friendly offers of assistance, he applied to me and to my religion the most opprobrious abuse, and treated me as if my Faith were inimical to the tenets of his Creed.

I am, your Friend and fellow-believer,
Ram Doss,
Calcutta, June 3, 1823.

---

[128] The full title reads: *A Vindication of the Incarnation of the Deity, as the common basis of Hindooism and Christianity against the schismatic attacks of* R. Tytler, Esq., M.D., Surgeon in the Hon. East India Company's Service, … and also, Member of the Asiatic Society. By Ram Doss, Calcutta: Printed by S. Smith and Co., Hurkaru Press, 1823.

RAMMOHUN ROY: A PUBLIC INTELLECTUAL.

INTRODUCTION

This Correspondence was occasioned by a passage in a letter of Dr. Tytler's published in the *Bengal Hurkaru* of the 30th of May 1823, directed against Rammohan Roy, a person who, as is well known, is strongly reprobated by the zealous both among Hindoos-and Christians, for his daring impiety in rejecting the doctrine of Divine Incarnations. But the Doctor while censuring this stubborn Heretic most unwarrantably introduced contemptuous allusions to the Hindoo Deities, as will be seen, from the passage referred to which is here subjoined :—

Extract from the Hurkaru —May 3^{rd,} 1823.
He (Rommohun Roy), thus proceeds in the same epistle. "Whether you be a faithful Believer in the Divinity of the Holy Lord and Saviour JESUS CHRIST, or of any other mortal man; or whether a Hindu declares himself a faithful believer in the Divinity of his Holy Thakoor Trata Ram or MUNOO—I feel equally indifferent about these notions." Here I pause, for the purpose of asking- the candid Reader what, would have been said, if, at the time Rammohan Roy continued in his belief of Siva, Vishnu and Ganesa, I had personally addressed a letter to him, replete with vituperation of him and his opinions? Would it not have been asserted, and very justly, that I was attacking him, and his gods, and wounding the religious feelings of a Hindu? Yet this Unitarian, as he now professes himself, thinks proper to leave the subject of discussion, namely a proposal to hold a "Religious conference" and tells me flatly that my belief in the Divinity of the Holy Saviour is on par with a Hindu's belief in his Thakoor!!! – Yes, Christian Readers, such is the fact; and when I offer to defend myself from such vile imputations by arguments drawn from those Holy Scriptures to which this Unitarian himself appeals, I am given to understand, that this Reviler of my FAITH, the FAITH OF MY ANCESTORS, will not condescend to listen, unless my reply receives the stamp of orthodoxy from the signature of a Missionary!!!

May 2, 1823.
R. Tytler.

RAM DOSS' FIRST LETTER TO DR. TYTLER.

The Editor of the *Hurkaru* having refused insertion to the following, it was privately forwarded to Dr. Tytler.

TAPATI BHARADWAJ

To, Dr. R. Tytler.

Sir,
I happened to read a Letter in the "Hurkaru" of the 3rd instant, under the signature of R. Tytler, which has excited my wonder and astonishment. For I had heard that you were not only profoundly versed in the knowledge of the ancients, but intimately acquainted with the learning and opinions of the present age. But I felt quite disappointed when I perceived that you entertained ideas so erroneous respecting the Hindoo religion.
Is there any Hindoo who would be offended at being told by a believer in the Invisible God that this man is indifferent about his (the Hindoo's) faith in the divinity of his Holy Thakoor or Trata Ram or Munoo? We know that these selfconceited sects who profess reverence for only one Deity are apt to express their indifference for the holy INCARNATION of the Divine Essence believed in by Hindoos as well as by Christians; and in fact that the followers of any one religion have little respect for the opinions of those of another. But can this give concern or surprise to the enlightened and well-informed persons who have seen and conversed with various sects of men?

I am more particularly astonished that a man of your reputed learning and acquirements, should be offended at the mention of the resemblance of your belief in the Divinity of Jesus Christy with a Hindoo's Belief in his Thakoor; because you ought to know that our religious faith and yours are founded on the same sacred basis, viz, the manifestation of God in the flesh without any restriction to a dark or fair complexion, large or small stature, long or short hair. You cannot surely be ignorant that the Divine Ram was the reputed son of Dasarath, of the offspring of Bhuggeeruth, of the tribe of Rughoo, as Jesus was the reputed son of Joseph, of the House of David of the Tribe of Judah. Ram was the King of the Rughoos and of Foreigners, while in like manner Jesus was King of the Jews and Gentiles. Both are stated in the respective sacred books handed down to us, to have performed very wonderful miracles and both ascended up to Heaven. Both were tempted by the Devil while on the earth, and both have been worshipped by millions up to the present day. Since God can be born of the Tribe of Judah how, I ask, is it impossible that he should be born of the Tribe of Rughoo, or of any other nation or race of men? And as the human form and feelings of Ram afford sceptics no good argument against his omnipresent and divine nature, it must be evident to you that this deluded sect of Unitarianism can lay no stress on the human form and feelings of Jesus Christ as disproving his divinity.

When therefore the resemblance is so very striking, and ought to be known to you as well as to every other man having the least pretensions to an acquaintance with the learning and religion of the Natives of India,—how is it possible that you can feel offended at the mention of a. fact so notorious? Yon may perhaps urge, that there is a wide difference between a belief in three Persons' in the Godhead as maintained by you, and a belief in three hundred and thirty millions of Persons in, the Godhead, entertained by the Hindoos. But as all such numerical objections are founded on the frail basis of human reason, which we well know is fallible, you must admit that the same omnipotence, which can make Three One and One Three, can equally reconcile the unity and Plurality of three hundred and thirty millions; both being supported by a sublime mystery which far transcends all human comprehension.

The vain and narrow-minded Believers in one Invisible God accuse the followers of the Trinity, as well as us the sincere worshippers of Ram and other Divine Incarnations, of being Idolaters; and policy therefore might have suggested to you the propriety of maintaining a good understanding and brotherhood among all who have correct notions of the manifestation of God in the flesh; that we may cordially join and go hand in hand, in opposing and if possible extirpating the abominable notion of a Single God, which strikes equally at the root of Hindooism and Christianity. However, it is not too late for you to reflect on your indiscretion, and atone for it by expressing your regret at having written and published anything calculated to create dissension among the worshippers of Divine Incarnations.

I am, Sir, Your most obedient Servant,
Ram Doss.

DR. TYTLER'S REPLY TO THE FOREGOING.

To Ram Doss,

I have received your letter and beg yon to receive my best thanks, for the trouble you have put yourself to in sending it to me. It was my intent on this evening to have proved that Hindu Idolatry and Unitarianism are the same, and that they both proceed from the Devil.—Unfortunately Mr. Robinson in consequence of the number who were anxious to attend, has requested me to postpone the meeting, to which of course I have acceded. But I am ready,— MIND ME, READY — to meet you and your runnagate friend Rammohun Roy, whenever you please, in public and private discussion, and let you know what a humble individual unsupported can do, armed with no other weapon than the sharp sword of the Gospel, in bringing to light the hidden works of darkness which are at present displayed in the damnable Heresy of Unitariantsm of which you are the wretched tool. But neither you, Rummohun Roy, nor the second fallen ADAM dare meet me because you fear the WORD of TRUTH.

Your inveterate and determined
foe in the LORD.
May Gift, 1823. (Signed) R. TYTLER.

RAM DOSS'S REPLY TO A REMARK OF THE EDITOR OF THE *BENGAL HURKARU*.

Sir,
To the Editor of the *Bengal Hurkaru*,

After publishing in your Paper of the 3rd instant Dr. Tytler's letter throwing out offensive insinuations against the Hindu Religion as unworthy to be compared with the Christian, I am truly astonished at your refusal to insert my very friendly Reply and expostulation with him for the error and indiscretion into which he has fallen, and that you moreover defend him in the following words: "We would hint to Ram Doss that there is in our opinion a wide difference between the belief which maintains God to have appeared in the Flesh and that of the Hindoo who believes the appearance of the omnipotent Being in the shape of a Thakoor, which if we "are not mistaken, is composed of stone, metal or wood."

I must remark, first, on the total unacquaintance, you have displayed, with the Hindoo Religion, notwithstanding your residence in the capital of Bengal, in which however you are more excusable than Dr. Tytler, considering his high pretensions to learning. Can you find a single Hindoo in the whole of India, who imagines that the divine Ram, the son of Dusruth by Koushilya his mother according to the flesh, was composed either of wood, stone or metal? If you can find even one, there may be some excuse for your mistake in supposing, what is so wide of the fact.— You may of course find numerous consecrated images or statues of the Holy Ram, in the Hindu temples, formed of wood and other materials, placed there for the pious purpose of attracting the attention of Devotees to that Divine Incarnation ;— although many good Hindoos do not consider such representations as necessary, and worship Ram directly without the intervention of any sensible object. But can you suppose for a moment that a model or picture o any person, whether divine or human, can identify that being with such representation or convert the original existence into the same materials? If this were the case, then the number of men so unfortunate as to have statues or portraits of themselves made, must lose their real essence—their original elements necessarily degenerating into stone, or paint and canvass.

But it is indisputable that neither the image of the Holy Jesus in Roman Catholic Churches, nor the representations of the Divine Ram in the Hindu Temples, are identified with either of those sacred persons.

As you have refused to publish my letter in answer to Dr. Tytler's attack, I shall take an opportunity of sending it directly to himself for his consideration and reply, and purpose very soon laying this controversy before the public through some other channel with proper mention of your partial conduct, in circulating Dr. Tytler's insulting insinuations against the Hindu Religion and withholding my answer thereto for its vindication. 1 expect you will kindly insert this letter in your Paper of tomorrow along with a justification of your own observations of this morning.

I am, Sir, your most obedient Servant,
Ram Doss.

REMARKS OF THE EDITOR RELATIVE TO THE FOREGOING
(Contained in the Bengal Hurkaru of the 8th May.)

In our subsequent pages will be found a letter signed Ram Doss, which we insert with pleasure, with a desire of convincing him that we are really impartial in our views of the subject of which it treats. In explanation of our refusal to insert the former letter of Ram Doss, we owe it to him to say that although it justly deserves, the appellation of a " very friendly reply" and although it was written with much ability, yet it appeared to us to overstep the limits we have prescribed to ourselves, by entering too far into the subject of the original dispute between the two classes of religious professors, instead of being confined to the discussion of the subject between Rammohun Roy and Dr. Tytler, namely the right of the latter to demand, and of the former to afford, facilities for the purpose of the discussion of the point at issue between them. It was under these circumstances and with this feeling that we are declined to insert Ram Doss's communication, and we beg to assure him that it was not from any disrespect to him, or partiality for Dr. Tytler or his doctrines.

Having disposed of this part of the subject we trust to the satisfaction of Ram Doss we shall simply remark on the other, that we never intended to Intimate that any sensible Hindoo could for one moment suppose that God was personally present in an image of brass, stone or metal; but we have no hesitation in asserting that such an opinion does prevail, not only among the Hindoos, but amongst the ignorant of all classes whose religious faith prescribes the worship of images as the medium of access to the Deity. We really ought not to enter on the discussion of any of the points connected with the religious worship of the Hindoos, as we have had but very few opportunities of making ourselves acquainted with them, and if we are now in any error on these subjects, we trust that Ram Doss will attribute it to the causes which we have thus explained, and not to any feeling of partiality towards Dr. Tytler, or of misrepresentation of the objects of his own worship.

RAM DOSS' FIRST CHALLENGE TO Dr. R. TYTLER,

To the Editor of the Bengal Hurkatu.

Sir,
Being disappointed in my just expectation of. having my answer to Dr. Tytler's insinuations inserted in your Paper, I yesterday sent it to the Doctor himself for his consideration; but he avoids making a reply thereto, and in answer to my arguments merely returns abuse against me, and likewise against our common enemies, the Unitarians, for which last I of course care nothing.

I take this opportunity of informing the Public that this Goliath, notwithstanding his high pretensions to learning, and presumption in setting himself up as the champion of Christianity, shrinks from the defence of the charges he has brought against Hindooism, and that he refuses to co-operate with me in opposing Unitarianism, although, he declares in his note to me - that it is a system of damnable heresy proceeding from the Devil.

I am, Sir, Your obedient Servant.
May 7, 1823.
Ram Doss.

DR. TYTLER'S REPLY TO RAM DOSS

To the Editor of the Bengal Hurkaru.

As I do not intend this letter to have any direct reference, to the subject of Religious discussion, you will oblige me by giving it insertion into the columns of the Hurkaru. Two day ago I received an Epistle subscribed Ram Doss which I was led to conclude must have been written by some Unitarian under a pseudonymous signature. But it appears from a letter, which is published in your paper of this day, 1 may have been mistaken; and I am, therefore, anxious to inform Ram Doss, if he be a real person, that I consider there is no book at present in possession of *Hindus*,—the *Mahabharat* and *Ramayuna* not excepted,—of higher antiquity than the entrance of the Mussulmans into- India,? say about 800 years from the present period. The legends attached to the *Avatars* are merely perverted, and corrupted copies of the Holy Scriptures in the possession of Christians, and have no particular relation to the ancient religion, whatever it may have been, of the inhabitants of this country. Should Ram Doss therefore be a real person, and wish to obtain information on those topics, it will afford me sincere pleasure to meet him, either at my own house or any other he may appoint, at some hour convenient to us both, for the purpose of explaining the arguments, which support the views I have taken of the *Modernness* of the religious system at, present followed by the Hindus.

Your obedient Servant,
May 8, 1833.
R. Tytler.

R.AM DOSS'S SECOND CHALLENGE TO DR. TYTLER.

To the Editor of the Bengal Hurkaru,

Sir,

Dr. Tytler haying been unable to make a direct reply to the arguments conveyed in my letter to him dated the 5th instant, has taken refuge in your Paper, knowing very well that, he would prevail upon you to insert every assertion that he might make against our Sacred Books and Holy incarnations, and that you as a Christian would excuse yourself for declining to give publicity to my retaliation, upon him.

I therefore challenge him through your Pages for a reply to my arguments in the shape of a letter, so that I may endeavour through some other means to publish all our correspondence for the consideration and judgment of the Public.

I am, Sir, your obedient Servant,

9th May, 1823.
Ram Doss.

DR. TYTLER'S REPLY TO RAM DOSS.

To the Editor of the Bengal Hurkaru.
Sir,

Your Correspondent Ram Doss in "informing the public" that I consider Unitarianism as a system of damnable heresy proceeding from the Devil" has forgot to mention that such was also my expressed opinion to him respecting the superstitions to which he is so extremely partial. Under those circumstances is it reasonable to expect, I will allow him to cooperate with me, as he calls it, "against our common enemies," when in fact I maintain *Unitarianism* to be nothing more than a new name for Hindoo Idolatry.

Your Obedient Servant,
Calcutta, May 10, 1823.
R. Tytler.

RAM DOSS' THIRD CHALLENGE TO DR. TYTLER

To the Editor of the Bengal Hurkaru.
Sir,

One of the objects of my Letter to Dr. Tytler, was to solicit the co-operation of the Doctor in opposing Unitarians. The other, to refute his insinuations against Hindooism and, prove that it was founded on the same sacred basis (the Manifestation of God in the flesh) with Doctor Tytler's own Faith.

From the Doctors letter in your paper of this morning, I see he positively shrinks from entering the field with me against Unitarianism, leaving me thus to encounter the danger and reap the glory single-handed.

I now request to be informed through the medium of your paper, whether the *Doctor* also flinches from justifying his insinuations against the Hindoo Religion, and replying to my letter proving Hindooism and Christianity to rest on the same sacred foundation.

I am, Sir,
Your obedt. Servt.
May 12th, 1823.
Ram Doss.

DR. TYTLER'S REPLY TO RAM DOSS.

To the Editor of the Bengal Hurkaru. .

Sir,

The assertion of Ram Doss that "I shrink from entering the field against Unitarianism, leaving him thus to encounter, the danger and reap the glory single handed," when all Calcutta is acquainted with the contrary, and no one better than the Unitarians themselves, is really too absurd to require notice.

In support of what this writer calls "my Insinuations against the Hindoo Religion," I refer him to the histories of *Buddha*, *Suluvahuna*, and *Chrishna*, and maintain they comprise nothing more than perverted copies of Christianity. Let him show the reverse if he can.

Your Obedient Servant,
Calcutta, May 13, 1823.
R. Tytler.

RAM DOSS'S REPLY TO THE FOREGOING.

To the Editor of the Bengal Hurkaru,
Sir,

You are aware that I have three times through the medium of your paper, called upon Dr. Tytler, to reply to the Arguments contained in the letter, forwarded to him by me and the receipt of which he acknowledged in a *torrent of abuse* and that he has as often as thus publicly called upon, returned an evasive answer, which proves that he inwardly shrinks from the combat.

With a view to defend his Offensive insinuations, against Hindooism, he now refers me to the Histories of Buddha (the head of a tribe inimical to Hindooism) Sulavahana (an Indian Prince) and Chrishna, a *divine Incarnation* without attempting to bring forward from these any thing against the justness of my arguments—I now, Sir, beg leave to appeal to you, whether if any Hindoo were to make insinuations against the Christian Religion, when called to defend them he would be justified in merely referring Christians to the Books of the Jews (a tribe equally in inimical to Christianity) or Gibbon's *History of the Roman Empire* or to a whole History of Jesus Christ, without adducing any particular Passage? I now for the Fourth and last time call upon the *Doctor,* either to answer precisely my arguments already in his possession, or confess publicly that he is totally unable to justify his insinuations against a Religion founded on the Sacred basis of the manifestation of God in the flesh, and that knowing the badness of his cause, he shrinks from meeting me on the fair field of *Regular Argument*, instead of which he has given me only abuse.

I have nothing to say respecting his mode of opposing our Common enemies the Unitarians, and grant him freely the honour of his individual exertions. Notwithstanding I think it is proper to suggest the expediency of Common believers in Divine incarnations (like the Doctor and myself) joining hand in hand in opposing our inveterate enemy. Our chance of success must be greater when our Force is united, than when it is divided.

I am, Sir, Your obedient Servant.
Ram Doss.
May 14th, 1823.

DR. TYTLER'S REPLY TO RAM DOSS.

This Reply was in a Postscript to a Letter of Dr. Tytler (dated May 15,) addressed to the Editor of the *Bengal Harkaru* and published in that Paper of the 16th May.

"I request" (said the Doctor) "to be informed by your sapient correspondent Ram Doss, in what manner he proves *Buddha* to be 'the head of a tribe' inimical to Hindooism."

RAM DOSS' REPLY TO THE FOREGOING.

To the Editor of the Bengal Hurkaru.

Sir,

The only reply which Dr. Tytler makes to my Fourth Challenge published in your paper
yesterday is as follows viz. -
P. S. I request to be informed by our sapient correspondent Ram Doss in what manner he proves Buddha to "be the head of a tribe inimical to Hindooism"?

I now call on the Public to pronounce whether this query can be considered as a reply to the arguments contained in my letter forwarded to the Doctor, repelling his offensive insinuations and proving that Hindooism and Christianity are founded on the same basis? or if it be not evidently a mere pretence for evading the question? Fully warranted in anticipating a verdict in my favor, I ask what opinion will the world form of a man who with some pretensions to learning and great professions of Religion, while defying the whole world in the field of Religious discussion, first utters degrading Insinuations against a Faith founded on exactly the same basis as his own, and then when repeatedly challenged to justify this conduct resorts to such *Shuffling* and *Evasion?* — However to oblige the Doctor as a fellow-believer in, and worshipper of Divine Incarnations, I will inform him (although it has no bearing on the question) that *Buddha* or *Booddha,* is the head of the sect of *Bauddhas,* who derive their name from him in the same manner as Christians do from Christ. That this sect is inimical to Hindooism is proved by the fact that they deny the existence of a Creator of the Universe, in whom the Hindoos believe, and also despise many of the Gods worshipped by the latter. There are hundreds of works published by them against each other which are in general circulation. But all this has nothing to do with my arguments which the Doctor by evading virtually confesses he is unable to answer. I therefore denounce him a defamer of

Hindooism, a religion of the principles of which he is (or at least appears to be) totally ignorant.

I am, Sir, your obedient servant,
Ram Doss.
Friday, 16th May, 1823.

DR. TYTLER'S REPLY TO THE FOREGOING.
Published in the *Harkaru* of May 22nd.

The sapient Ram Doss now changes his tone,—and tells us the *Buddhists* "despise many of the Gods worshipped by the Hindoos." It hence follows that *some* of the Hindoo deities must be objects of their adoration. And yet this writer asserts *Buddha* to be the " head of a tribe inimical to Hindooism "while his own statement proves Hindoo Gods to be the objects of *Buddhaic* veneration !!.

RAM DOSS' REPLY TO THE FOREGOING.

To the Editor of the Bengal Hurkaru,

In your paper of this day, Dr. Tytler notices my fifth challenge, calling upon him to answer the arguments contained in my letter forwarded to him some weeks ago, repelling his offensive insinuations against Hindooism — But how does he justify himself? "The sapient Ram Doss" (says he) "now changes his tone and tells us "the Buddhists despise many *of* the Gods worshipped by the Hindoos." It hence follows that *some* of the Hindoo deities must be objects of their adoration—And yet this writer asserts Buddha to be the head of a tribe inimical to Hindooism, while his own statement proves Hindoo Gods to be the objects of Buddhaic veneration.

I now beg to call the attention of the Public, Christians and not Christians to the above passage, and request them to pronounce whether the Doctor thereby proves that Hindooism cannot (as insinuated) be compared with Christianity, or refutes my position, that these two religious are founded on the same sacred basis, viz the Manifestation of God in the Flesh? and I now call on the world to judge, whether the person who can resort to such shuffling and evasion have any just claim to the character of a man of learning, or a man of probity? –What name is bestowed on the man who thus shrinks from meeting the arguments of his opponent fairly and candidly, and trembling at the force of truth, is glad to make his escape by any mean subterfuge?

It is almost self-degradation or a prostitution of reason to treat his last remark, above-quoted, as worthy of notice, viz- that as "Buddhists despise many of the Gods worshipped by the Hindoos, it hence follows that *some* of the Hindoo deities Must be subjects of their "adoration." *Indeed!* In what school of wisdom did the learned Doctor acquire his Logic? Although I *despise* or dislike several members of a family, is this a proof that I must adore the rest? May I not regard the rest with indifference, or be unacquainted with them? But granting even that Buddhists do worship *some* of the Hindoo Gods, while they despise others, may they not still be inimical *to* Hindooism? For, don't the Jews despise one of the Christian God's, worship another, and are indifferent to a third; and yet are they not inveterate enemies of Christianity?

I now only wish to know from what College or University the Doctor procured a Certificate, authorizing him to assume the Title of *M. D.* and whether that seat of Learning in the distribution of its *Academic Honors usually* selects such worthy subjects?

I am, Sir, Your obedient Servant.
Ram Doss.
Thursday, 22nd May 1823.

P. S. I congratulate the Doctor On his Victory (as reported by himself in your paper of today) over our common enemies the Unitarians (these deluded deniers of Divine Incarnation), and I regret I was present to share in the triumph. - R. D.

Dr. Tytler being now, it appears, completely silenced, a Friend under the signature of A Christian, came forward to his assistance in the following Letter.

LETTER OF A CHRISTIAN TO RAM DOSS

To the Editor of the Bengal Hurkaru,

It is gratifying to the lovers of science to behold a few intelligent Hindoos emerging from the degraded ignorance and shameful superstition in which their fathers for so many centuries have been buried. It is no less pleasing to the friends of humanity, to find that one of the most learned of the Hindoo

Brahmins has not only abandoned the doctrine which countenances the cruel and abominable practice of matricide, but also ably confuted his compeers, who were advocates for having human victims sacrificed to Moloch.

On the other hand it is a sad contemplation, that these very individuals who are indebted to Christians for the civil liberty they enjoy, as well as for the rays of intelligence now beginning to dawn on them, should in the most ungenerous manner insult their benefactors by endeavouring to degrade their religion, for no other reason, but because they cannot comprehend its sublime Mysteries.

My attention has been particularly attracted to this subject by a letter signed Ram Doss which appeared in your paper of yesterday.

This Hindoo with whom I have no personal acquaintance had the arrogance to lay before the public the following passage "I now call on the *public* to pronounce whether this query can be considered as a reply to the arguments contained in my letter forwarded to the Doctor, repelling his offensive insinuations and proving that *Hindooism and Christianity* are founded on the same basis?" Ram Doss here appeals to the public, and he will ofcourse grant me the same privilege. I will therefore ask,— Christian Readers, are you so far degraded by Asiatic effeminacy as to behold with indifference your holy and immaculate Religion thus degraded by having it placed on an equality with Hindooism—with rank idolatry— with disgraceful ignorance and shameful superstition?

Will Ram Doss or his associates be pleased to inform me, if the *Incarnation of his God* was foretold by Prophets through a period of four thousand years? Or will he demonstrate the mission or divine incarnation of his *Deity* by incontestable and stupendous miracles such as Christ wrought? Will he assert that the doctrine of Hindooism is as pure and undefiled as that of Christianity? Or in fine will he prove that the human character has ever been exalted by any religious system so much as by the sweet influence of Christianity?

If Ram Doss is not able satisfactorily to clear up a single point of what I now submit to his serious consideration, it is manifest, that in common civility, he should refrain from insulting Christians by putting their religion on a comparison with Hindooism.

Rammohun Roy, who appears to me to be the most learned of the Hindoos, is so far from making such odious and offensive remarks, that he apparently gives the preference to Christianity. Vide, his First Appeal entitled "the precepts of Christ the guide to peace and happiness." I regret the learned Brahmin was interrupted by the intemperate zeal of the Baptists the praise-worthy course he intended to have pursued as set forth in his preface to the work above alluded to.

I conclude by recommending your sapient Correspondent Ram Doss to employ his time and talents in laudable and pious endeavors to reclaim his Countrymen from idolatory, rather than to investigate mysteries that are far above the weak comprehensions of man. I also recommend him to beware of such Christians as are carried away with every wind of doctrine, and who know not what they do.

I am, Sir, your Obedient Servant,
A Christian.

RAM DOSS' REPLY TO THE CHRISTIAN.
[Published in a Pamphlet containing an account of Dr. Tytler's Lecture circulated with the *Bengal Hurkaru* Newspaper.]

Sir,
To the Editor of the Bengal Hurkaru.

I regret to observe by the Letter in your Paper of this morning signed A Christian that in repelling the offensive insinuations of Dr. Tytler against the Hindoo Religion, I am considered by one of the Christian denomination as endeavouring to degrade his *faith*.
It is well known to you, Sir, that I privately sent a Letter to the Doctor, refuting his position in the most friendly, calm, and argumentative manner, to which he returned a note loading me with the grossest abuse; consequently I thought myself justified in challenging him publicly to make a reply to my arguments. The Christian therefore cannot conceal from himself that it is *I* and *my* Faith which have been vilified and abused, and that in return I have offered *not* insult, but merely reason and argument; for it cannot be considered insult for a man to say that another religion is founded on the same basis with his own, which he believes to be all that is venerable and sacred.

If by the "Ray of Intelligence" for which the Christian says we are indebted to the English, he means the introduction of useful mechanical arts, I am ready to express my assent and also my gratitude; but with respect to *Science, Literature or Religion,* I do not acknowledge that we are placed under any obligation. For by a reference to history it may be proved that the World was indebted to *our ancestors* for the first dawn of knowledge, which sprung up in the East, and thanks to the Goddess of Wisdom, we have still a philosophical and copious language of our own which distinguishes us from other nations, who cannot express scientific or abstract ideas without borrowing the language of foreigners.

Rammohun Roy's abandonment of Hindoo doctrines (as "A Christian" mentions) cannot prove them to be erroneous; no more than the rejections of the Christian Religion by hundreds of persons who were originally Christians and more learned than Rammohun Roy, proves the fallacy of Christianity. We Hindoos regard him in the same light a Christians do Hume, Voltaire, Gibbon and other Sceptics.

Before "A Christian" indulged in a tirade about person's being "degraded by *Asiatic* effeminacy" he should have recollected that almost all the ancient prophets and. patriarchs venerated by Christians, nay even Jesus Christ himself, a Divine Incarnation and the *founder* of the Christian Faith, were ASIATICS, so that if a Christian thinks it degrading to be born or to reside in *Asia,* he directly reflects upon them.

First—The *Christian* demands "Will Ram Doss or his associates be pleased to inform me if the *Incarnation of his God* was foretold by Prophets through a period of four thousand years?" I answer in the affirmative. The Incarnation of Ram was foretold in the works of many holy and inspired men for more than 4000 years previous to the event, in the most precise and intelligible language; not in those ambiguous and equivocal terms found in the *Old Testament,* respecting the Incarnation of Jesus Christ, an ambiguity which it is well known has afforded our common enemies the Unitarians a handle for raising a doubt of Jesus Christ being a real Manifestation of God in the flesh. " . '

Secondly—The Christian demands of Ram Doss "Will he demonstrate the mission or divine incarnation of his deity by incontestable and Stupendous Miracles such as Christ wrought?" I answer, Yes: The divine Ram performed miracles more stupendous, not before multitudes of ignorant people only, but in the presence of Princes and of thousands of learned men, and of those who were inimical to Hindooism. I admit that the Jains and other unbelievers ascribed Ram's miraculous power to a Demoniacal Spirit, in the same manner as the Jews attributed the miracles of Jesus to the power of Beelzebub; but neither of these objections are worthy of notice from believers in Divine Incarnations; since the performance of the miracles themselves is incontestably proved, by tradition.

Thirdly,—The Christian asks, "Will he (Ram Doss) assert that the Doctrine of Hindooism is as pure and undefiled as that of Christianity?" Undoubtedly, such is my assertion: and an English translation of the Vedant as well as of Munoo (which contains the essences of the whole Veds) being before the public, I call on reflecting men to compare the two religions together, and point out in what respect the one excels the other in purity? Should the Christian attempt to ridicule some part of the ritual of the Veds I shall of course feel myself justified in referring to ceremonies of a similar character in the Christian Scriptures; and if he dwell on the corrupt notions introduced into Hindooism in more modern times, I shall also remind him of the corruptions introduced by various sects into Christianity. But A *Christian* must know very well that such corruptions cannot detract from the excellence of Genuine Religions themselves.

Fourthly.—The Christian asks, "Will he (Ram Doss) prove that the human character has ever been exalted by any system of religion so much as by the sweet influence of Christianity." In reply, I appeal to History, and call upon the Christian to mention any religion on the face of the earth that has been the cause of so much war and bloodshed, cruelty and oppression for so many hundred years as this whose *"sweet influence"* he celebrates.

That propriety of conduct found among the better sort of Christians is entirely owing to the superior education they have enjoyed; a proof of which is, that others of the same rank in society, although not believers in Christianity are distinguished by equal propriety of conduct, which is not the case with the most firm believers, if destitute of Education or without the means of improvement by mixing in company with persons better instructed than themselves.

It is unjust is the Christian to quarrel with Hindoos because (he says) they cannot comprehend the sublime mystery of his Religion; since he is equally unable to comprehend the sublime mysteries of ours, and since, both these mysteries equally transcend the human understanding, one cannot be preferred to the other.

Let us however return to the main question, viz. that THE INCARNATION OF THE DEITY IS THE COMMON BASIS OF HINDOOISM AND CHRISTIANITY. If the manifestation of God in the flesh is possible such possibility cannot reasonably be confined to Judea or Ayodhya, for God has undoubtedly the power of manifesting himself in either country, and of assuming any colour or name he pleases. If it is impossible, as our common enemies the Unitarians contend, such impossibility must extend to all places and persons. I trust therefore the Christian will reflect with great seriousness on this subject and will be kind enough to let me know the result.

I am, Sir, your most Obedient Servant,
Ram Doss.
Calcutta, May 23,1823.

Ram Doss having heard nothing more publicly or privately from Dr. Tytler or "A Christian" the correspondence here concluded, and the arguments adduced in vindication of the Incarnation of the Deity as the Common Basis of Hindooism and Christianity consequently remain unanswered.
FINIS.

TAPATI BHARADWAJ

www.ingramcontent.com/pod-product-compliance
Lightning Source LLC
Chambersburg PA
CBHW071737040426
42446CB00012B/2391